IMAGES
of America

LATINOS IN WAUKESHA

Antonia Don Diego Melendes was born on October 9, 1900, in Aguascalientes, Mexico. At age 13 she married Joseph Melendes, aged 25, and soon settled in Waukesha. During World War II, she worked at General Castings, Arlan's Shoe Store, and Leilani's Restaurant. Antonia was a member of the Guadalupe Society at St. Joseph's Church and of the Christian Mothers. The Melendes home was known for its welcoming spirit, where families would gather, and there was never a shortage of tortillas and frijoles.

On the cover: A group of women competed for the title of festival queen at the Mexican Independence Day celebration. The event was held in the former sales pavilion on Baxter Street, which was as an auction hall for cattle. As one of the few spaces that rented to Mexicans for parties, the place was cleaned up for the event, which included music, dancing, and entertainment. Many Latinos remember the hall as *el salon de las vacas*, "the hall of the cows." Attending the event in 1946, from left to right, are (first row) Jovita Lugo García and Connie García; (second row) Olivia Arreazola, Isidra Mindiola García, Raquel "Rachel" Arreazola Pérez, Isabel García Arreazola, Socorro Llanas Torres, Josefina Saldivar, and Guadalupe Saldivar. (Courtesy of La Casa de Esperanza.)

IMAGES
of America

LATINOS IN WAUKESHA

Walter Sava, Ph.D., and Anselmo Villarreal

ARCADIA
PUBLISHING

Published by Arcadia Publishing
Charleston, South Carolina

Library of Congress Catalog Card Number: 2007932092

For all general information contact Arcadia Publishing at:
Telephone 843-853-2070
Fax 843-853-0044
E-mail sales@arcadiapublishing.com
For customer service and orders:
Toll-Free 1-888-313-2665

Visit us on the Internet at www.arcadiapublishing.com

To History Builders founders, Kenneth and Clair Crouch,
Duane and Pat Mitchell, and Duane and Carol Warren,
the padrinos "sponsors" of La Casa de Esperanza, Inc.
—Walter Sava, Ph.D.

To my dearest friend, Marty H. Frank.
—Anselmo Villarreal

CONTENTS

ACKNOWLEDGMENTS

Through the combined efforts of a variety of people, this book aims to achieve its goal of documenting the history of Latinos in Waukesha, sharing their contributions, and celebrating the Latino culture and heritage.

Our astounding collection of historic photographs was made possible by several residents of Waukesha who were eager to embrace the project and share their family histories. We would especially like to thank Walter and Pedro Llanas, Margie Ollalo, Pedro and Virginia Rodríguez, Rev. Joe Medina, Virginia Hernández, Mary Banda Casper, Dolores Banda Gourda, Nancy Hernández, and Estela Camacho for their photographs. Thank you to the Waukesha County Historical Society and Museum, the Milwaukee Journal Sentinel, the Waukesha Freeman, and St. Joseph's Church for permission to use their wonderful photographs.

We would also like to thank Juan Darío Lara for his dedication in the research and restoration of the photographs; his time was invaluable. Many thanks to Erin Neary and Rebecca Cabrera for their help in revising and editing much of the text. We would also like to thank many of the La Casa de Esperanza employees, such as Terrie Peret, Shari Campbell, and Carmen de la Paz for providing insight into the project.

This project was funded in part by grants from the Greater Milwaukee Foundation, Hispanics in Philanthropy, and the Wisconsin Humanities Council, with funds from National Endowment for the Humanities. The Wisconsin Humanities Council supports public programs that engage the people of Wisconsin in the exploration of human cultures, ideas, and values.

We extend a special thanks to all those who shared their family stories and photographs. We are happy they chose to celebrate and treasure their own history. Finally, we are continuously grateful to our Latino ancestors. Their hard work and persistence are what makes Waukesha's Latino community what it is today and what inspires today's Latinos to embrace their heritage while carving out their own future.

INTRODUCTION

Latinos began arriving in Waukesha in the 1920s and 1930s. Many of them came through Texas and other Midwestern states, often employed as migrant workers. They worked in the north during summer and in Texas during winter, where the climate remained more constant. However, when the workforce began to move out of the fields and into the factories, many Latinos decided to permanently settle in Waukesha. Initially some families moved onto a street in Waukesha called the Strand, which soon became identified as a solid Latino community. Other families lived in a shantytown area by the Highway 164 quarry. Soon these Latinos formed what became a growing community and started to adapt to life in Waukesha.

This book tells their stories: families that came to Waukesha with hardly anything but the clothes on their backs were able to secure factory work or other jobs, raise a family, and become solid members of the community. Their children would grow up to be outstanding citizens: school board members, teachers, police officers, and military heroes. These families continue to succeed, but not without their share of obstacles. Latinos in Waukesha have frequently encountered racism and discrimination, particularly from civic officials who are unwilling to meet the growing needs of this population. This is an ongoing struggle, but the strength and resolve of Latinos will ultimately win out.

The photographs and stories included here aim to be a representative snapshot of the Latino presence in Waukesha. It is estimated there are now 15,000 Latino residents in Waukesha County, and about 10 percent of the population in the city of Waukesha is Latino. The images and voices of Waukesha's Latino community came together to share their personal and family stories through this book. It is a testament to their strength, success against incredible odds, and perseverance through trying times. The Latinos in Waukesha have become community leaders, businesspeople, and activists. We look to them to lead the Waukesha community forward and guide the next generation of Latinos.

The original White Rock School was built in 1891 on White Rock Avenue, close to Main Street. It was enlarged in 1924, and by the late 1940s, with an enrollment of more than 200 students, it had difficulty accommodating the increasing number of Latinos. As plans were formulated in 1948 to build a new school by Frame Park, there was concern by city officials that "pupils will eventually be walking long distances to attend classes in a bad smelling section of the city." Eventually the school board prevailed, and the new White Rock School was inaugurated in 1951.

Two decades after the first train ran from Milwaukee to Waukesha, the Williams Street passenger depot opened in 1875. It was one of three Waukesha stations to serve the Chicago and Northwestern route, nicknamed "the 400" for the travel time between Chicago and Minneapolis. Abandoned in 1949, it became several different restaurants during the 1970s. Owner Tony Márquez has since remodeled the old station into a Mexican restaurant, La Estación.

One

THE STRAND

At first glance, the Strand is typical of any other street in Waukesha. But upon closer examination, the Strand is revealed as the heart of Waukesha's Latino community. The Melendes family arrived in Waukesha in 1919 and settled into what had originally been an Italian neighborhood called the Strand. The Strand would become an intermixture of cultures, which is evidenced by the Italian, Mexican, and Puerto Rican groceries sold at the Strand Market.

Initially the Melendes family could not afford to buy their house so they cleverly turned it into a boardinghouse. The boardinghouse provided needed income for the family, as well as an inexpensive place for new immigrants to sleep. Boardinghouses and neighborhood bars, such as the Strand Bar, were examples of the entrepreneurial spirit found in many ethnic neighborhoods. Despite the lack of asphalt and city investment in the Strand, it was one of the first areas in the city of Waukesha where Latinos were able to become homeowners. Although many of the houses on the Strand were small, they offered decent-sized lands and good-sized yards for families. This affordable housing was also near farmlands and foundries, such as International Harvester, where many Latinos worked. The Strand was more than just a neighborhood, it was a place where individuals found a sense of community away from their original homelands. Many residents settled in the Strand area because the neighbors spoke their language, shared their food, and understood their culture.

The Strand continues to be a place where many second- or third-generation Latinos reside. There continues to be an ever-present sense of spirit, pride, and culture. In 2006, the first Latinos in Waukesha, the Melendes family, were honored with a street in their name. Upon receiving this recognition, a third-generation family member noted that he would rather an alley be named in honor of the family. The alley, unlike the street, was the main point of entrance for individuals who lived in the Strand. Calle Melendes represented the walk from the Waukesha area to the cultural neighborhood many Latinos called home.

The first home in Waukesha owned by a Mexican family was purchased by the Melendes family and located on 1105 the Strand. Joseph Angel and Antonia Don Diego Melendes moved to Waukesha in 1919, and although they were listed in the official census of 1920, they did not officially own the home until February 1928. By boarding other Spanish-speaking individuals in their home, the Melendes family assisted newly arrived immigrants to transition into the local workforce.

Joseph Angel Melendes was born in Penjamo, Guanajuato, Mexico, on March 19, 1888, and arrived in Waukesha at the age of 31. He was one of the founders of the Sociedad Mutualista Hispano Azteca, a group dedicated to helping newly arrived Mexicans. He became a U.S. citizen on May 1, 1944. Pictured here is Joseph (left) with a friend, wearing pistolero outfits during a visit home in his later years.

The backyard of the Melendes home at 1105 the Strand was the setting for many family pictures. Primitivo (Primo) Melendes, on the right, posed in the 1920s with Sam Martinez, who is wearing his Sunday best.

Another branch of the Melendes family is that of Jésus María Vásquez and Soledad Melendes Vásquez. The couple is pictured on the Borden Farm in Wharton, Texas, shortly before Soledad's brothers moved up north and settled in Waukesha in 1919.

Leonard "Pro" Melendes, son of Joseph and Antonia Melendes, was born while the family was transitioning between Mexico, Iowa, Minnesota, and finally Waukesha. Pro is pictured on the far left with workers at Wisconsin Centrifugal, his employer until retirement. His employee identification card from General Malleable Corporations reads, "This employee is a citizen of the United States as established by records filed with this company." He is considered the first Latino to have graduated from Waukesha High School and was the first to run for alderman during the April 1, 1952, election.

The Melendes family has a history of helping people in need. Antonia was like a midwife to newly arrived families who could not access hospital care. Their home was used as a funeral home, where wakes could be conducted. During the Depression, some of the priests from St. Joseph's Church stayed with the family. Immigrants looking for work stayed in the home, a part of which was used as a rooming house. Pictured in 1985 are, from left to right, (first row) Richard Hernández, Antonia Melendes, and Carrie Hernández; (second row) Daniel Melendes and Joseph Melendes, sons of Joseph and Antonia.

María Refugio Vásquez came from Saltillo, Mexico, to San Pablo, Texas, where she met Pedro Villareal. They married in 1937 and settled in Waukesha on the Strand in 1940. Like many other Latino families in Waukesha, they continued the Mexican tradition of picnics in the parks. Pictured above are María and Pedro in 1940, visiting Holy Hill with their children Richard and Stella. They had four more children: Joseph, Daniel, Mary Christine, and Arlene.

All six Villareal children attended Waukesha public schools and graduated high school. Pictured by their house on the Strand in the late 1940s are, from left to right, Joe, Richard, Daniel, and Stella. Joe and Richard served in the army. Joe worked for the U.S. post office and served as president of La Casa de Esperanza's board of directors. Richard owned a beauty salon. Daniel became an alcohol and drug counselor, and Stella worked for 30 years at Walgreen's.

Margarito "Henry" García (right) is pictured with his parents, Enrique and Jésus. The family came from Texas and settled in Waukesha in the 1940s. Henry has lived most of his life with his wife, Olivia, and four children on the Strand. The building on the right is Heale Manufacturing, where he has worked for 50 years, and at age 70, he is still working today.

Emilia Zamarripa Arreazola was born in Zacatecas, Mexico. Her family migrated to New Brunfels, Texas, to work in the cotton fields. Pictured at right in the mid-1940s, Emilia is remembered as kind and religious. She enjoyed staging *pastorelas* (short plays dealing with a religious event), was an outstanding *zobadora* (massage giver), and an expert *ventosa* applicator (small glasses that would be swiped with alcohol, lit, and quickly placed upside down on the back of the patient).

14

Six-year-old Richard Hernández (front, center) is enjoying an afternoon with his siblings, cousin, and family friend on the porch of his grandparents' home at the Strand in September 1945. Seated from left to right are Víctor (Richard's brother who served in the National Guard along with Richard), his sister Cecilia, and Richard. In the back is a visiting family friend on leave from the armed services and cousin David Melendes.

Female employment increased significantly during the mid-1940s, particularly in the foundries that were involved with the war effort, and Waukesha was no exception. At the International Harvester factory, Latina female employees began entering the workforce in significant numbers. Pictured here, in the first row, are Margarita García (left) and Olivia Arreazola (right).

Richard Hernández (first row, second from right) is pictured with his cousins and friends in 1945 on the Strand. The area around the Strand was largely neglected by the City of Waukesha until the late 1970s. Mayor Joseph C. LaPorte targeted this neighborhood for major rehabilitation, which included curbs, pavement, and other needed improvements.

Nepotism was a common hiring practice of many local foundries. Members of the same family would work at the same place and encourage other family members, who may still be living in Texas, to move to Waukesha. Pedro Rodríguez came to Waukesha when he was 17 and ended up working with his brothers-in-law and sisters-in-law at International Harvester. In Texas, he was working for a pittance at a gas station for 10 hours a day, seven days a week. Pictured above are, from left to right, Salvador García, Pedro Rodríguez, Margarita García Salazar, and Frank García.

The integration of Mexicans into mainstream Waukesha society often manifested itself in sports and recreational activities. Area foundries would sponsor softball teams and bowling leagues, where participants ended up socializing with each other. This 1950s photograph of the International Harvester bowling league includes several Latinos, among them are Baldo Sánchez, Frank García, Angelo Llanas, Chico Hurtado, Margarita García, and Salvador García.

Rich's Strand was the baseball team sponsored by Rich's Bar at the corner of Perkins Street and the Strand. Kneeling in front of the trophy is Leonard Hernández, who came to Waukesha in 1926 from Robstown, Texas. Also pictured in the second row are (third from left) Lorenzo Anzivino, (fourth from left) George Renna, (fifth from left) Leonard "Pro" Melendes, (third from right) Alexander "Alex" Melendes, and (far right) Mateo "Matt" González.

In September 1961, Crescenciano Arreazola hosted a get-together for his sons and sons-in-law at his home at 1200 the Strand. Standing from left to right are Pedro Llanas (son-in-law), Juan José "John Joseph" Arreazola, Crescenciano (the patriarch of the Arreazola family), Aureliano, Benito Rodríguez (son-in-law), and Benito A. García (son-in-law).

Mary Gonzáles Hernández was born in Olwein, Iowa, on April 13, 1917, and married Leonard at age 20. They lived most of their lives at 908 Regent Street in the Strand area and were the parents of seven children. The couple was active at St. Joseph's Church and at La Casa de Esperanza. Mary was known for her tortilla-making skills and made any fiesta truly memorable.

Two sisters, Soledad Melendes Vásquez (left) and Ursula Melendes Banda, are matriarchs of two of Waukesha's oldest Latino families. These two women count among their descendants some of Waukesha's more prominent and productive Latino residents.

Baseball was a favorite pastime for many of the men that lived on the Strand. Pictured above in this c. 1940s photograph are, from left to right, (laying) Perfecto Hernández; (first row) Ed Rodríguez, Frank González, Leon Llanas, Joe Medina, Leonard Hernández, and Solomon González; (second row) Tom Montez, Pro Melendes, Leo Julio Maldonazo, Joe Hernández, Mick Mesa, Cruz Juarez, and Pete Villarreal.

One of Waukesha's most popular institutions was Mindy's Tap on the Strand. Ophelia and Stanley Mindiola operated this tavern from 1981 to 2005. Very popular for its Mexican food, it received the Best Tacos in Town award from *Milwaukee Magazine*. The Mindiolas have lived in Waukesha for more than 50 years and are the parents of seven children.

This photograph is one of the last taken of Antonia Melendes (center) at her home on the Strand, before she moved to a nursing home. On the left is Enrique Martínez, who came to Waukesha from Guanajuato in 1920 and lived in Doña Antonia's house for some time, and on the right is her niece Mary Banda Casper, who currently lives in Pewaukee.

Many Latino families were disappointed when an alley behind the Strand was renamed Calle Melendes because they hoped a major thoroughfare or avenue would receive the Melendes designation. Many do not know that naming an alley in honor of a Latino family was not a slight by the City of Waukesha officials, but was a direct response to a letter from Joseph A. Melendes. The former Waukesha city attorney exemplified the humble and compassionate spirit of the entire Melendes family when he wrote, "I find the naming of this alley as a fitting tribute to my grandfather and grandmother who came to the city in 1919. Throughout my lifetime, in recollection of my contact with them, they were very humble, caring and nurturing individuals." A *Waukesha Freeman* article captured the true meaning of the alley when it stated, "For many Hispanic immigrants, the alley behind The Strand leading to the door of Joseph and Antonia Melendes was a path to a new life."

Many of the families who originally settled in the Strand area continue to live there. The parents may no longer be there, but their children are. This 1958 picture shows siblings and friends who grew up in the area that many still call home. Pictured above from left to right are (first row) Margarita "Margie" Marchan Olallo, who still lives in the house she grew up in on Raymond Street and has worked at La Casa de Esperanza for more than 20 years; David García, who also still lives on Raymond Street and works at Navistar; and Lydia Tovar, who also still lives on Raymond Street and has been working at La Casa for the past two years; (second row) Frank J. Marchan and Sylvia García, who served on the board of directors of La Casa in the early 1980s; Sandra Rodríguez, a registered nurse working at St. Joseph's clinic; Beatrice García, who works for the Wisconsin Department of Health and Human Services; and José "Joe" Rodríguez, who works for Milwaukee County as a case worker and is married to Jean and has four boys.

Two

Latinos Then

Waukesha seemed an unlikely place for both Mexicans and Puerto Ricans due to the cold climate and lack of acculturation, yet they were drawn to Waukesha because of jobs and affordable housing. Many Latinos in Waukesha were recruited from Texas to work in the farmlands and later in the foundries on the outskirts of the city. Migrants worked on a variety of fruit, vegetable, grain crops, and sugar beet fields. This recruitment was intensified during World War II, when Waukesha needed civilian workers for the factories. Many women, including Latinas, were able to work in the factories at this time. Other Latinos served their country in the military, and some even gained American citizenship through their service. Along with decent-paying jobs, the city of Waukesha offered cheaper land and larger houses than those available in larger cities such as Milwaukee and Chicago. Even though many Latinos lived in substandard living conditions, many were content with good location, low rent, and big backyards.

While many of the first Latinos resided in the Strand, others lived in ramshackle housing in a neighborhood alongside the Highway 164 quarry. These houses were surrounded by railroads, highways, and trees; and the neighborhood consisted of about two dozen rental units that were the property of the Waukesha Lime and Stone Company. The rental houses were built to house quarry employees, and rent was only $40 a month, which was cheaper than rent in the city at $100 a month. In 1968, the neighborhood was razed due to freeway expansion. With only 90 days to relocate, individuals were displaced, and many moved back to Texas or relocated elsewhere.

Factory work was hard and arduous and so sports, music, and spending time with family provided many Latinos some necessary recreational time. Baseball was a favorite pastime, and many factories even had their own coed baseball teams. Many Latinos also attended *bailes* or dances at places such as *el salon de las vacas*, or the hall of the cows. These dances and pastimes provided Latinos with a distraction from the tough and demanding realities of their everyday lives and work.

In December 1921, Amador Llanas (right) paid "coyote" border smugglers $5 to help his family cross into Texas. They ended up in Lockhart, where his brothers Bibiano (left) and Marcos (center) were working on the Buhrmann farm. Under an arrangement called *medieros*, the owner provided the land and tools, and the workers provided the labor. They split the proceeds 50/50, but in the meantime, they were expected to make most of their purchases at the company store.

Most Latinos in the 1920s were on their way to or from a nearby state and ended up in Waukesha. Pictured as they were heading north, while laying sewer pipes in Iowa for the Moore-Sieg Construction Company in the early 20th century, are (first row, third from right) Primo Melendes, (fourth from right) Joseph Melendes, and (fifth from right) Leonardo Banda. Standing in overalls, behind Joseph, is Pio Torres.

In 1917, Leonardo Giatan Banda (left) immigrated to the United States from Yrapuato, Guanajuato, Mexico, with his friend Pio Torres (right). Soon Banda found work laying sewer pipes for the Moore-Sieg Construction Company of Waterloo, Iowa, with his future brothers-in-law, Joseph and Primo Melendes. In 1919, Banda settled in Waukesha and soon began work at Werra Aluminum Foundry as a molder. By 1923, he was working for Quality Aluminum Casting Company, where he stayed for 25 years.

Salvador García, born in Zamora, Michoacán, Mexico, came to Alido, Texas, in the 1920s. He was drafted into the army and became a U.S. citizen while serving in the European theater for four years. Upon his return he came to Waukesha, where his parents had moved. García retired from International Harvester and was involved with the VFW. He was one of the first presidents of the Mexican American Scholarship Fund and a lifetime member of the Eagles Club.

This 1931 photograph of students at St. Joseph's Catholic School includes Alex Melendes (second row, fourth from right), Mary Gonzalez, and Carmen Melendes (third row, second and third from right). Very few Latino families were able to send their children to St. Joseph's School until the 1960s.

The Hidalgo basketball team was sponsored by St. Joseph's Church. This picture was taken around 1930 and includes, from left to right, (first row) Frank González, Rey Fuentes, Leonard "Pro" Melendes, Leonard Hernández, and Alex Melendes; (second row) the parish priest, one of the twin brothers who was a boarder with the Melendes family, Matt González, George Hernández, the other unidentified twin brother, Matt Hernández, and coach Mugs Inzeo.

Carmen Melendes, daughter of Joseph and Antonia, was born in Minnesota in 1918. After coming to Waukesha, she married George Hernández in 1936. The couple had four children: Víctor, Richard, Cecilia, and Carrie. Carmen was a teacher's aide at Blair School and a volunteer and teacher's aide at La Casa de Esperanza's Escuelita. Among her many awards was the YWCA Woman of the Year Award.

The García children posed before the family automobile in Alido, Texas, in the late 1930s. Their father, Enrique, worked for the railroad but was told to move north as a migrant worker so his son could get a draft deferment from World War II. The García family moved to Wisconsin, but the son was sent overseas anyway. After settling in Waukesha, many worked for International Harvester. Pictured above are, from left to right, María, Josefina, and Aurelia, with Margarito "Henry" in front.

Leonard Hernández came to Waukesha with his family in 1925 with a trainload of Mexicans bound for work in Michigan, searching for a better life than their days of picking cotton in Texas. The family eventually ended up in Waukesha, where Hernández entered first grade at White Rock School at age 11. When he was in fifth grade, at age 15, teachers sent him to Waukesha's vocational school. "I was told I was too big." Hernández has lived most of his life in the Strand area neighborhood. He and his wife, Mary, also the child of Mexican immigrant parents, raised nine children there. Hernández was employed in Milwaukee by the Ladish Company, where he retired after 25 years. "We were one of the first Mexican families here," he said. They arrived about 2:00 in the afternoon, and his father had a foundry job by 9:00 the next morning, Hernández said. Pictured above are Leonard and Mary on their wedding day, April 17, 1937, at St. Joseph's Church. These quotes from Hernández are courtesy of a *Waukesha Freeman* article, March 21, 1983.

Sugar beets were a popular crop in Green Bay, where members of the Villareal family spent many summers. Pictured above in 1938 are, from left to right, Hortensia Ojeda "Tia Tencha," Pedro Villareal, María de Jesús Monreal "Chuy," Catarino Monreal, and Simón Monreal.

One characteristic of Latinos who moved to Wisconsin was the close relationship between friends and relatives. Many came because a friend or relative facilitated the move. Pictured at right in Green Bay in 1938 are, from left to right, Manuel San Miguel (a friend of the Villareal family), Raymond Ojeda (brother-in-law of Pedro Villareal), and Pedro. Standing in front is Raymond Jr., known in Waukesha for starting the rock-and-roll band El Rey and the Night Beats.

Mary González Hernández, with daughter Dolores in her arms, sits next to her mother, Nicolasa González, in this 1940 photograph. Sitting on the far right is María López. Nicolasa was born in Mexico, and for a time the family worked on the railroad, traveled by rail, and lived in railroad cars.

In the early 1940s, Don José Jiménez, who had been living in the shantytown around the Highway F quarry, moved his family to an area now known as Highway 59 and Arcadian Avenue. At the time there was a small pond, and the area was used to dispose of old streetcars. The permanent home of José and now his son Lupe is unrecognizable compared to earlier pictures. Pictured above is José (right) with his daughter Socorro (third from left) and her friends.

José Jimenez shared with Wally Llanas, Waukesha's unofficial Latino historian, the atrocities committed by Pancho Villa in Mexico, which included shooting his enemies and hanging them from trees and telephone poles. José witnessed the Battle of Celaya in 1914, where Gen. Alvaro Obregon defeated Pancho Villa, and was moved by the odor of death throughout the city. On December 24, 2000, Don José died at age 101, the oldest Latino resident of Waukesha.

Waukesha's Frame Park was a favorite gathering place for Latino families and served as a nostalgic reminder of Mexico's "parques and plazas." It was also a great setting for taking family photographs, which went to family and friends back home. Tomas Montes and his wife, María de Jesús Montes, enjoyed this outing in the early 1940s with their children Rita and Tom Jr.

Arcadio Ramírez was inducted into the U.S. Army in 1943. He is pictured above in Europe, shortly before the end of World War II.

Wally Llanas has written an interesting series of unpublished essays about his brothers in the military. Fernando was drafted in 1944 and inducted into the air force, serving the U.S. mainland. Twins John and Chris received their draft notice in 1942. Chris (pictured at right) served the army in France in 1944, while John served in the air corps in Iceland. Pedro served in Japan in 1948, and their brother Paul went to Korea in 1953.

Born in Kennendale, Texas, Frank García came to Wisconsin in 1943 and joined the army the following year. He served in the 89th Infantry Division in Europe during World War II. He was an avid bowler and bowled a 300 game in 1971. García was a lifetime member of the VFW and retired from International Harvester.

Going to downtown Waukesha for an afternoon at the movies was a favorite pastime of the Llanas sisters. All three have been longtime residents of Waukesha and came to Wisconsin as migrant workers. Pictured at left in 1945 are, from left to right, Janie Llanas Marchan, Socorro Llanas Torres, and María Llanas Márquez. Janie recently retired from Industrial Towel and Uniform. Socorro was an avid baseball player throughout her youth. María has lived in the same house for the past 50 years and enjoys listening to the rock-and-roll group Rockin' Robins, which includes her sons, Mario and Freddie.

Latina baseball teams often incorporated amusing elements into the game, such as the donkey ride, when players would ride to base atop each other. This 1940s photograph is of the "Texans Team," which included Jovita Lugo, Sara López Mesa, Willie García López, Isabel García Arreazola, Connie García, Margarita García Salazar, Virginia Monreal Hurtado, Elena Hernández, María Llanas Márquez, Olivia Arreazola, José Fuentez, and Socorro Llanas Torres.

Some families supplemented their earnings by renting rooms or beds to boarders. Others set up in-home restaurants where boarders would have a main meal, purchased on a weekly or monthly basis. The Hernández family left Nuevo Leon, Mexico, in 1912 and eventually arrived in Waukesha in 1927. Pictured at left, from left to right, are Inez, Anita, Joseph, and Trino Hernández, who along with their parents Juan and Sefarina helped with the in-home restaurant operated by one of their relatives.

Trino Hernández posed for this 1947 picture in what was then known as "the pit," a swimming hole. The hole, in the area of Estberg and West Avenue, eventually became a garbage dump, over which an apartment complex was built. By 2005, the apartments became uninhabitable because of methane gas contamination from the dump, and the buildings were demolished.

Socorro Llanas Torres is surrounded by her bridesmaids on her wedding day, April 17, 1948. Standing from left to right are Rachel Arreazola, Isidra Mindiola García, Socorro, Virginia Monreal Hurtado, and Margarita García Salazar.

Almost one-third of the students in Mary Jane McCarragher's class at White Rock School in 1950 were Latino. Pictured above is the last fourth-grade class to have attended the old White Rock School (in the background). Among some of the Latinos students above are Bartola Ramos, Gloria Hernández, Lupe Lugo, Martha Munõz, Virginia García, Mary Ojeda, and Bonnie González.

Entertainment venues for Latinos were limited. In the summer, a popular gathering place was the Arcadian Inn, a campground where large numbers of Latinos could hold a dance or have a picnic. This facility was popular well into the 1960s. Pictured above in 1951 are the Jiménez girls on their way to a party. From left to right are Felisa, Louis, Eva, Elizabeth, Socorro, Esther, and little Rosie in the front.

The Latino softball teams in the 1950s frequently included Anglo members who had befriended or who were interested in meeting the Latina girls. Included in this group at Buchner Park are Marcos López, Lupe Jiménez, Eddie Gámez, Margarita García Salazar, and Angelo Llanas.

Lupe Jiménez was born in Waukesha in 1930, and his parents were among the first families to have settled here. Shortly after graduating from Waukesha High School, he entered the military and served with the 1st Marine Division in South Korea between 1951 and 1953. He is pictured here (left) with a friend. Upon his return from service he worked for Quality Aluminum, where he retired after 31 years of employment.

Cpl. Marcos "Jessie" Martínez volunteered to join the armed services in 1948 and served in the Korean War. A letter from the Department of the Army issued on January 11, 1951, informed his parents, "your son, Private First Class Marcos Martínez, RA 16283876, Artillery, has been reported missing in action in Korea since 6 December 1950." The letter further states, "missing in action is used only to indicate that the whereabouts or status of an individual is not immediately known." After being held as a prisoner of war from December 6, 1950, to August 18, 1953, the Martinez family received news that Marcos "was released from a Communist prison camp in North Korea after the signing of the armistice, rests in Inchon, Korea, before boarding the ship which will take him home." Pictured above are, from left to right, Andrea Méndez (sister), Rita Martínez (grandmother), Ester Méndez McHargue (niece), Epifanio Martínez (father), and Atanasia Martínez (mother), as they receive news of Marcos's release.

Cpl. Marcos Martínez received a warm welcome when he returned to Waukesha after 985 days as a prisoner of war. In 1953, the city of Waukesha held a parade to welcome him home. Riding with his father, Epifanio, Marcos was the recipient of various gifts and public recognition. In 1988, he was awarded a Prisoner of War Medal, but it was not until 2000 that he finally received a Purple Heart.

Janie Llanas Marchan (second row, center) enjoyed her bridal shower in 1953 with her coworkers at Walgreen's. The Walgreen's and the Woolworth store, both on Main Street, were popular shopping destinations for many Latinos.

Mary Banda Casper (third from left), daughter of Ursula and Leonard Banda, worked for Warren O'Brien Commercial Photographer in downtown Waukesha. She was a darkroom lab technician. This 1954 picture is typical of the photography studios of that time, where many Latino families would have their family portrait taken by professional photographers.

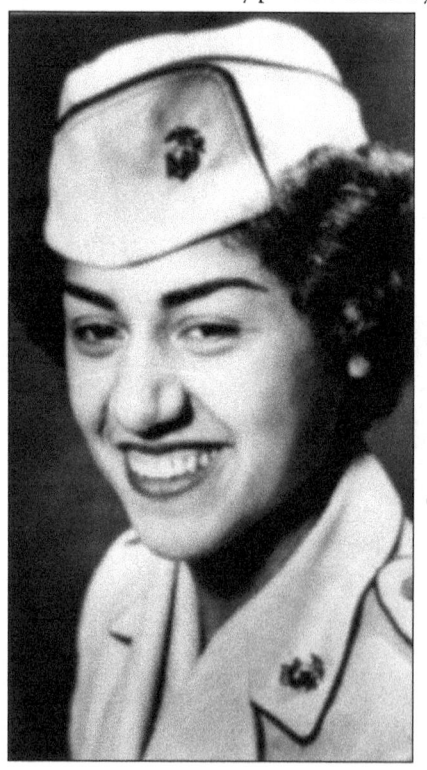

Esther Veronica Jiménez Finn joined the U.S. Marines in the mid-1950s. After graduating from Waukesha High School, she worked in the veterinary offices of Dr. David Roberts and decided she wanted to see the world. She is pictured in the new marine uniform for women. According to a story in the *Waukesha Freeman*, it was "made of Dacron, considered then a miracle fabric that would dry quickly after laundering and required no ironing."

The Strand is commonly associated with the area of Waukesha where there was a high concentration of Latinos and some of the earlier families settled. Another area that has been largely forgotten is Highway 164 and J (now F). This 1910 photograph includes some of the 24 rental units owned by Waukesha Lime and Stone that were originally built to house quarry employees. In the 1950s and 1960s, they were rented to Latino families. Rev. Joe Medina remembers living in the area as a child and was instrumental in obtaining a copy of this photograph, courtesy of Tim Hackett from Payne and Dolan Aggregates. A newspaper article from November 1969 includes interviews with Susie Medina and Sam Nicosia, as the houses were scheduled for demolition to make way for the expansion of Highway 161. They lamented the loss of their homes, which they rented for about $40 a month.

In the 1940s, many Latinos came to the city because of labor shortages. Migrant families resettled in the area, and some were encouraged to come from as far as Jamaica to work in the foundries. Soon adequate housing became a major issue, and after the war, the government recognized the housing shortages. Pictured above in 1955 are Steve Gonzalez (left) and Trino Hernández (right). The Veteran's Administration built a housing complex of 20 buildings where the Virginia nursing home is currently located.

Waukesha Latino residents of 50 or more years fondly remember the parties, dances, and picnics held at the Arcadian Inn Park, at present-day Greenfield Avenue in the New Berlin area. Pictured above in July 1959 are Felisa Jiménez, with a child on her lap, and Jessie Montez, looking on. This private facility had several characteristics of Mexican parks where families could spend an afternoon or evening unencumbered by noise or drinking ordinances.

Family pictures made in the shape of postcards were very common in Mexico. Miguel Ocampo (far right) is enjoying an afternoon with his friends in Buena Vista de Cuellar, Guerrero, in the late 1950s. The postcard was mailed to friends and relatives.

Inez Robert Llanas came to Waukesha from south Texas in the 1940s. He graduated from Waukesha High School and married Carmen Castillo in 1954. Carmen was one of the first Latina graduates of Catholic Memorial High School. Inez served in the U.S. Air Force in Korea and was the first Latino mail carrier in the city of Waukesha, where he worked for 26 years.

Typical of Mexican families with Texas roots was a change, abbreviation, or transformation of the first name. Pictured above at a birthday party for Jimmy Salazar are, from left to right, Salvador "Sal" García Sr., Margarito "Henry" García, Enrique García, and Francisco "Frank" García. Only Enrique, the Mexican-born father of Sal, Henry, and Frank, continued using the name given to him at birth.

44

The García sisters were known not only for their beauty, but also for their voices. They were frequent guests at various church festivals and events where they would sing, accompanied by Aurelia "Willie" on the guitar and other instruments. Pictured from left to right are Margarita Salazar, Josefina Hernández, María García San Miguel Benavides, Willie López, and Virginia Rodríguez.

Gloria Sandoval Rozman is well known for her beauty, charm, and talent. She entered several beauty pageants in the early 1960s, including the Miss Milwaukee contest and the Milwaukee Spring Horse Show at State Fair Park. Pictured above is Gloria, with her escort Carlos Sevilla as the king and queen of the 1962 Festival of Our Lady of Guadalupe Church in Milwaukee.

Living conditions for some Latinos were often similar to those they experienced before coming to Waukesha. The Jiménez home did not have indoor plumbing or heat until 1963. Latinos looked forward to summer when family and friends would visit, pitch a tent, and stay for the weekend. The women gathered in the kitchen and prepared their favorites dishes while the men played cards and told stories.

The tradition of military service is strong among Latino families. It was not uncommon to have several brothers serve at the same time. Also, different generations served in different wars. Pictured above is Henry Martínez (right), nephew of Joseph Melendes, who served in World War II, and his son Leland, who served in Vietnam. Henry was born in Mexico, but his son is a Waukesha native who is now retired.

Sgt. Vicente de la Paz from Puerto Rico served in the U.S. Army from 1964 to 1966 and was stationed for a year in Vietnam, where this picture was taken. Later Vicente visited his father in Waukesha and decided to stay. Vicente was a fourth-degree member of the Caballeros de Colon and secretary of the Vietnam Veterans, Chapter 425. He was also an active La Casa de Esperanza volunteer, where he organized the domino league and bowling teams.

Among the leading Latino activists in Waukesha during the 1960s and 1970s was Armando García. He served on the board of La Casa de Esperanza in the early years and was active on the City of Waukesha Equal Opportunities Commission. He is best known for his recruitment of Latino students at Waukesha County Technical College, where he worked for about 20 years, until his retirement in 1990. (Courtesy of the Waukesha County Historical Society and Museum.)

Pedro and Virginia Rodríguez have been Waukesha residents since the 1960s. They will soon be celebrating their 50th wedding anniversary. Pedro worked for International Harvester and attended the University of Wisconsin-Milwaukee. He also became executive director of La Casa de Esperanza. He spent most of his professional life working for the State of Wisconsin, and Virginia was one of the first Latinas employed by Wisconsin Natural Gas. They both recently retired.

Lucio Benavides, born in Texas of Mexican parents, graduated from Arrowhead High School in Hartland. He became the first Latino firefighter in the Waukesha Fire Department in 1966. Historically both the fire and the police departments of the city of Waukesha have excluded Latinos in their employment practices. Benavides retired on December 31, 1996, with the rank of deputy chief.

Three

FAMILIES

Certain characteristics epitomize the Latino culture: work, faith, and *familia* or "family." For Latinos everything revolves around family, and it is the reason many individuals relocated or chose to stay in Waukesha. Many Latinos did not directly come to Waukesha from Mexico, but migrated from states such as Minnesota, Arkansas, and Texas. When relatives would visit their families in Waukesha, many chose to stay so that they could be closer to their families. To help one another financially, many of these extended families resided in the same households. Also, many families were employed by the same companies and worked together for many years.

Latino families came to the United States just like many other immigrant groups did around the same time in search of jobs, housing, and the hope that their children's future would be more prosperous than their own. Some families came to the United States because of the economic disparity and political turmoil found in their native countries. After the collapse of the Puerto Rican sugar industry in the 1950s, many Puerto Ricans migrated to the United States in search of better jobs. Other Latin American groups such as Nicaraguans left due to political turmoil in their country.

The foundation of Latino families has always been religion, which is still true today. Religion, especially Catholicism, provided the moral foundation for many Latinos. Many Catholic Latinos were married in churches, and if they had the money, they would send their children to parochial schools like St. Joseph's. Work, faith, and family continue to be important aspects of the Latino spirit. Family and religion provided the foundation that helped Latinos survive and succeed in Waukesha, which was far from their native land and very different than their own. To this day family is of utmost importance and is celebrated in reunions across Waukesha. These gatherings are essential to bring together first, second, and third generations to celebrate their heritage, culture, and family.

Magdalena Gómez Melendes married Joseph M. Melendes in 1879. She was only 13 years old at that time. They raised tobacco on their ranch in Penjemo, Guanajuato, Mexico. Joseph and Magdalena had nine children, of which the following five lived at one time or another in Waukesha: Ursula Melendes Banda, Joseph A. Melendes, Primitivo "Primo" Melendes, Soledad Vasquez, and Perfecta Ramires. This photograph is from the early 1900s.

This photograph of Antonia Melendes and her brother Matt González was taken around 1915, shortly after Antonia got married in Clinton, Iowa, before continuing to Minnesota on their way to Waukesha. Antonia's parents were Nicolasa Castañeda, from Mexico, and Esperon Don Diego, from Spain.

This early-1920s photograph includes three of the Melendes children. Pictured in their Sunday best are, from left to right, Carmen, Leonard "Pro," and Alex.

In 1930, Alex Melendes was the only student of Mexican heritage in the St. Joseph's School band. Standing on the far right, in the first row, is 14-year-old Alex.

This 1936 photograph continues the chronicle of the Melendes family with the arrival of their latest child, David. Pictured at left is baby David in the arms of his mother, Antonia Melendes, and in the second row, from left to right, are Carmen, Leonard "Pro," and Alex.

The Melendes family is widely regarded as the first Mexican family to have moved to Waukesha. Pictured in this c. 1950 photograph are, from left to right, (first row) Antonia, David, and Joseph; (second row) Alex, Carmen, and Pro.

Among the first Mexican families to come to Waukesha were Ursula Melendes Banda and her husband, Leonardo Banda. Ursula was born in 1903 in Abasolo, Mexico. In 1917, her mother, Magdalena Melendes, died and Ursula's brothers, Joseph and Primo, promised to take care of her. The siblings traveled to Minnesota and finally settled in Waukesha in 1919. Pictured in this 1930 photograph are Ursula, Leonardo, and their children (from left to right) Dolores, Mary, and Reuben.

Carmen Melendes and Perfecto Hernández took their marriage vows at Our Lady of Guadalupe Church in Milwaukee on May 23, 1936. Perfecto came from Aguascalientes, Mexico, and Carmen was born in Minnesota, shortly before her parents came to Waukesha. Perfecto was a molder at Waukesha Foundry, International Harvester, and General Castings. They had four children, including Richard, who became Waukesha's first Latino alderman in the 15th District.

Pictured above at the Borden Farm in Wharton, Texas, is the Vásquez family, shortly before they moved to Waukesha in 1943. Shown from left to right are Leonard, Vinino, Jésus María Vásquez, Jésus "Jessie," Soledad (holding Frank "Pancho"), Juana, and Quirina "Chila," twin sister of Vinino. Chila later married Manuel Oyervides.

Amador Llanas came to Texas in 1921 and later established family roots in Waukesha. His wife, Rosa, had left many relatives in Mexico, and every few years a family portrait was taken to share with them. Pictured above in the 1950s, from left to right, are (first row) Juana "Janie," Rosa, Carlos "Charlie," Amador, and María Jesús "Susie"; (second row) Baltazar "Wally," María "Mary," Fidela, Socorro, and Isidro "Chilo"; (third row) Inez, Chris, Angelo, John, Pedro, and Paul.

54

When Rosa Balandran Llanas crossed the Rio Grande in December 1921, she was pregnant with twins who were born a few weeks later. Pictured here is Rosa with her children, from left to right, Socorro Llanas Torres, Juan "John," and Cristóbal "Chris." Rosa and her husband, Amador, were the parents of 15 children.

The Llanas family is one of the largest in Waukesha. Pictured above, from left to right, are Charlie Llanas, his cousin Richard Torres, and cousin Ronald. Charlie still resides in Waukesha. Richard lives with his wife, María, in Dousman. Ronald served in the Vietnam War in the army. He and his wife, Katie, have been longtime Waukesha residents. Ronald retired from Wisconsin Centrifugal and was active in managing and supporting the city softball program.

Two large families were joined when Olivia Arreazola married Pedro Llanas on June 23, 1951. Pictured above are the parents of the bride and groom, Crescenciano and Emilia Arreazola (left), and Rosa and Amador Llanas (right). Olivia, one of six girls in her family, was the first to graduate high school and the first to get married. She retired from Waukesha County Technical College, and Pedro retired from International Harvester.

There are several interesting elements related to the annual Llanas family reunions. Family T-shirts are common to distinguish geographical regions. Nametags are needed to keep up with the various family additions. Pictured above in 2000 are, from left to right, (first row) Susie, Fidela, Socorro, Janie, Daria, Mary, Panchita, and Fernando; (second row) Angelo, Chilo, Pedro, Simón, unidentified, Victoria, Octavio, Walter, Johnny, Viviano Jr., Paul, Alicia, unidentified, Eugene, cousin Inez, and Inez.

Doña Rosa Llanas, aged 77, and Don Amador Llanas, aged 83, celebrated their 62nd wedding anniversary at La Casa de Esperanza's senior center in 1980. They came to Waukesha in 1943 and worked in various farms, including sugar beet farms in Green Bay. Amador retired from Waukesha's International Harvester, and during their retirement days they were faithful members of La Casa's senior center. (Courtesy of the Waukesha County Historical Society and Museum.)

Emilia Arreazola was the mother of 12 children, of which two died as infants and two (including Daniel, at right) passed away in their teens. Infant mortality was rather high for many of the migrant families who had little access to health care.

The severe labor shortage during World War II caused International Harvester to search the Iron Ridge area for possible employees. The Arreazola families worked in sugar beet migrant camps but were convinced to move to Waukesha. Pictured in the mid-1940s are, from left to right, Juan José "John Joseph," Aureliano, Emilia, and Crescenciano in front. Aureliano retired from International Harvester, and Crescenciano retired from General Malleable Corporation.

A family portrait of the Arreazola "children" taken in the early 1980s includes, from left to right, (first row) Mary, Raquel "Rachel," Aureliano, and Isabel Chevela; (second row) Emilia "Emily," John Joseph, Graciela "Gracie," and Olivia. John was one of the first Latino graduates of Carroll College in 1955 and went on to earn a doctorate.

Don José Jiménez, with his wife, Felisa, and daughter Rose, took this photograph in the mid-1940s. He left Mexico in 1917, when railroad companies were recruiting people to work on the rails for $16 a week (about 22¢ per hour). The work was seasonal, so he could go back and forth to his hometown in Celaya. After they married in 1922, José and Felisa moved to Chicago and later Waukesha. The family was among the earliest settlers of the shantytown on Highway 164 (today Highway F).

José and Felisa Jiménez had eight children, seven girls and one boy. They all graduated from high school. José was famous for his huge garden, where he grew all types of vegetables for the family, friends, and for sale. He guarded it with a shotgun, claiming it was to help keep intruders out, but everyone knew it was to "protect" his daughters, including Socorro Jiménez Garza, pictured above.

This 1980s photograph of the Jiménez "girls" includes, from left to right, Esther Finn Secora Garza, Elizabeth Monreal, Anna Cantu, Lupe Jiménez, Felisa Jiménez, José Jiménez, Mary González, Rose Chacón, and Eva Lugo.

Evaristo Alonzo Marchan and Margarita Contreras were married in Laredo, Texas, in 1927 after coming from Durango, Mexico. Margarita was an excellent cook who stayed home to take care of their six boys and three girls. The family worked as migrant workers until finally settling in Waukesha in the 1950s. Most of the Marchan brothers worked in local foundries. Don Evaristo and Doña Margarita were married 61 years.

Evaristo Marchan came to the Waukesha area in the early 1950s from Texas to work on the farms in Palmyra. He enjoyed telling stories of his days in Pancho Villa's army and worked in various capacities at La Casa de Esperanza well into his 70s. Pictured from left to right are (first row) Santiago, Doña Margarita, Evaristo, Don Evaristo, and José; (second row) Josefina, Guadalupe, Juanita, and María. Not pictured are sons Francisco and Tomas.

Evaristo Marchan (second from right) came with his parents, Evaristo and Margarita, to the Waukesha area in the 1950s via Durango, Mexico, and Laredo, Texas. He is very proud of his children, featured from left to right, Leonel, Lupita, Javier, and Arturo. Evaristo is a strong supporter of La Casa de Esperanza and a frequent volunteer at various La Casa events. His children are all professionals with a strong sense of community service.

This 1959 picture of the Marchan family includes Jane Llanas Marchan and Francisco Marchan, with their children, from left to right, Caroline Marchan Caraballa, Frank J., and Margie Marchan Olallo. The children still live in Waukesha. Margie has been working at La Casa de Esperanza for the past 22 years, while Caroline works for Accents on Hair Design, and Frank works for Schlossmans Auto Imports.

Felix and Micaela Mireles migrated from Crystal City, Texas, to Racine in the early 1950s to raise their 12 children. Several Latino nonprofit agencies have benefited from the enthusiasm and dedication of the Mireles children, including the Spanish Center in Racine, the United Community Center, and La Casa de Esperanza. The United Community Center was well served when Oscar was the associate executive director in the 1990s. He is currently executive director of Omega, in Madison. Jesús, or "Jesse," is the human services manager with Waukesha County and has been a La Casa board member since 1989. He is currently the board president and a driving force behind La Casa's growth and expansion. Pictured in the first row, from left to right, are Jesse, Oscar, Raquel, Felix Jr., and Víctor. Not pictured are oldest brother, Julian, and youngest sister, Juanita.

The formality of studio pictures taken in the 1930s is reflected in this portrait of the Garcia children. Pictured from left to right are Sal, Frank, and Margarita "Marge."

The Sandoval family, with roots in Aguascalientes, Mexico, and New Mexico, came to the Milwaukee area in 1941. Pictured with her parents and siblings is Gloria Sandoval Rozman on her wedding day in December 1964. Gloria has lived in Waukesha for more than 30 years and has operated a variety of business with her late husband Vern, including Gray Lumber and a hardware store. Gloria and her three children, Rachel, Phillip, and Suzanne, currently own the Cabinet Place.

Henry García came to Waukesha from Alido, Texas, while his wife, Olivia, was from Carrizo Springs, Texas. Both of their families were migrants, traveling from Texas to Arkansas and to the Midwest. The couple met at a community event in Milwaukee. They have lived most of their married life on the Strand. The couple is featured in this 1964 picture with their children, from left to right, Daniel, Margo, and Sandy. Their son Randy is not pictured.

Hortensia and Ramón Ojeda came from Mexico to Waukesha via Texas and Green Bay. They moved to the Strand in 1942 and had six children. Pictured above are, from left to right, (first row) Hortensia, Corrine, and Ramón; (second row) Margarita, Rubén, Raymond "Ray," Henry, and María. Ray was the most musically inclined child and eventually formed the El Rey and the Night Beats music group.

Manuel Oyervides and his wife, Chila Vásquez Oyervides, came to Waukesha in 1943 from Seguin, Texas. They were a very prominent couple in Waukesha's Latino community. Manuel operated a television and radio repair shop, and after retiring, he established Save and Save, La Tienda Mexicana on the first floor of his White Rock home. He volunteered at St. Joseph's Church, La Casa de Esperanza, served on Waukesha's Equal Opportunities Commission and the Fire and Police Commission, and was president of LULAC (League of United Latin American Citizens). Pictured above are, from left to right, (first row) Irma O. Galindo, Chila Oyervides, and Jane Oyervides; (second row) Manuel Michael Oyervides Jr. and Manuel Oyervides.

Arcadio Ramírez came to Waukesha after serving during World War II. He was La Casa's Volunteer of the Year in 1988. Pictured in this family portrait are, from left to right, (first row), Rebecca (who received her doctorate from the University of Wisconsin-Madison); Arcadio; his wife, Margarita; and Andrew (a police lieutenant in Hartland); (second row) Daniel (who works with a local manufacturer); Arthur (a labor organizer); and Ralph (a Waukesha circuit court judge).

Dolores and Eddie Gámez came to Wisconsin from Texas in the late 1940s and lived on the Strand with their nine children. Eddie served in the National Guard and retired from International Harvester after 36 years. Pictured above, from left to right, is their family (first row) Tito, Kate, Linda, and Jackie; (second row) Anna Marie, Dolores, Eddie, Christina, and Dolores; (third row) Debra, Fred, Roberto, Richard, and Margaret; (fourth row) Eddie Jr. and Diane.

Florinda Rodríguez met Luis R. Hernández in Crystal City, Texas. They married in 1951 and came to Wind Lake as migrant workers, eventually settling in Waukesha. Luis retired from International Harvester, and Florinda from Waukesha Rubber Company. In addition to raising their nine children, they were faithful volunteers at St. Joseph's Church and La Casa de Esperanza, and spearheaded the efforts of the Scholastic Fund for Students of Hispanic Descent.

The Hernández family took the above 1975 photograph in their Waukesha home. Pictured are, from left to right, (first row) Yolanda, Florinda, Cesar, and Luis Sr.; (second row) Anito and Armando; (third row) Hector, Rosalva Cruz, Luis Jr., Julia, and Henry. Both Luis and Florinda had a fifth-grade education but succeeded in ensuring their children receive high school diplomas. Several even pursued higher degrees.

Sandy and Luis Barrera came to Waukesha in the mid-1950s. Sandy has been employed by La Casa for about 30 years and is the program coordinator of La Casa Village. She was a member of the City of Waukesha Planning Commission, Fair Housing Commission, and the Waukesha County Department of Senior Services committee. Sandy and Luis have four children, Daniel and Geraldine (pictured here) and Anna and Tom.

José Angel Medina (right) stands with his son, Oscar, and compadre, Pete. José spent his early years picking cotton in Lubbock, Texas, and other various farms. The family came to Waukesha in the late 1950s and settled north of the city (around Highways F and JJ) where a quarry still operates. The area had a small shantytown of Latino families, many of whom worked for Owens Farms. Most of the houses have since been razed.

Born in Vicente Guerrero, Durango, Mexico, Angela Marchan came to Waukesha in 1957. She was married to Guadalupe Marchan in 1958, and they had five children. Angela was one of the first students to attend English classes at La Casa de Esperanza at the Ryan Street location in the late 1960s. Angela still resides in Waukesha and spends time with her grandchildren, sharing stories about the family's experiences while adapting to Waukesha.

The Rodríguez family posed for this 1970s photograph. Standing in the first row, from left to right, are Gloria, Pedro, and Alicia; (second row) María, Crescenciana, Armijo, Evangeline, Irene, Juan, Sylvia, and Cirilo Jr.; (third row) Dardomiano Armijo, Cirilo, and Braulio. María is a poll worker, Alicia was the first Latina elected to the Waukesha County Board of Supervisors in 2000, and various members of the family have been involved in Waukesha's Latino community and civic life.

Rafael Gutiérrez came to Waukesha in the early 1960s from Puerto Rico and worked as a bilingual parent coordinator for Waukesha Public Schools during the early 1970s. He went on to become director of University of the Wisconsin-Milwaukee's Spanish Speaking Outreach Institute and was a strong voice for the Puerto Rican community. With Rafael are his children, from left to right, Rolando, Vilma, Marisol, Anaida, and Sigfredo "Fred."

Vicente and Carmen de la Paz met on a blind date and got married in 1965. Two years later, they moved to Waukesha from San Juan, Puerto Rico. They are pictured here with their children, Carmen and Vicente Jr. in 2001. The de la Paz family has been actively involved in the Latino community. The elder Vicente was a wonderful supporter and volunteer at La Casa, where his wife Carmen was the director of the preschool program Escuelita.

In 1968, Miguel and María Ocampo immigrated from Guerrero, Mexico, to Waukesha. Searching for better opportunities, they worked in foundries, hotels, and factories. Pictured from left to right are (first row) Dimas Ocampo, Dimas Arizmendi, Dolores Arizmendi, Dolores Ocampo Brown, María Ocampo, Miguel Ocampo, and Judy Ocampo Uribe; (second row) Zulema Ocampo Hauer, Miguel Angel Ocampo, and Luz Arizmendi. All five Ocampo children graduated from Escuelita, St. Joseph's Elementary School, Catholic Memorial High School, and Carroll College.

During the 1970s, Mayor Paul Vrakas of Waukesha was a strong supporter of the Waukesha-Granada (Nicaragua) Sister City Program, which sought to strengthen the sociocultural ties between the two cities. Among the more obvious manifestations of this program were the Nicaraguan artists who visited Waukesha, Carroll College students who participated in Nicaraguan baseball tournaments, and student exchange programs. Several families from Granada ultimately immigrated to Waukesha, including the Benavente, Brautigan, and González families.

The González family immigrated to Waukesha from Granada, Nicaragua, in the mid-1970s to escape political turmoil. Several family members, upon arriving in Waukesha, worked at Paul Vrakas's Metropolitan Restaurant. Today they are all productive members of Waukesha's Latino community and have been affiliated with La Casa de Esperanza in various capacities. Pictured above are (first row) R. Tatiana (left) and María José; (standing) Alvaro, Julia, Roberto, Roberto Jr., Cristina, and Mario.

The Lazcano family came to Waukesha from Durango, Mexico, in 1976. Pictured from left to right are (first row) Sylvia, Epifanio, Leonila, and Richard; (second row) Francisco, Maria Dolores, Juan Luis, and Ruben. Epifanio worked for General Castings Corporation, and Leonila spent several years with Friday Canning in Sussex. Francisco, the oldest son, served in the U.S. Marines from 1995 to 1999 and is currently a police officer with the City of Palmyra Police Department.

Judge Ness Flores's parents came to Wisconsin as migrant workers from Texas. His many firsts include first Latino appointed judge in Wisconsin, first Latino elected judge in Waukesha County, first Latino member of the Wisconsin Public Service Commission, and first Latino appointed to the University of Wisconsin System Board of Regents. Picture above is his family, from left to right, (first row) Adrian and Kyra; (second row) Ben, Ness, Phylis, Carlos, Jenica, and Bart.

Four

LATINOS NOW

The first Latino immigrants in Waukesha paved the way for future generations. Their hard work in the foundries and farmlands led to increased economic advancement, educational success, and business opportunities for Latinos today. Many of the first Latinos came to the United States with little more than an elementary education. Gaining an education was an important precept of many Latino families. Where many early Latinos did not even go to high school, Latinos today are graduating high school, college, and even pursuing further education. Today Latinos have become exceptional teachers, lawyers, and even judges. The second generation exceeded its parents' expectations, and many chose to serve their country through military service or civic services such as law enforcement. Other Latinos have held notable offices in Waukesha County, such as circuit court judge, sheriff, alderman, and school board member. Some Latinos chose more artistic endeavors, such as becoming filmmakers and musicians. Music has always held a great influence on the Latino culture. *Conjuntos, bandas,* and *grupos musicales* from the Waukesha area have entertained at many social and community events throughout the years. These musical groups represent the Tejano musical influences and traditions still seen today. Other musicians like the Rockin' Robins and El Rey and the Night Beats, one of the longest-running bands in Wisconsin, played rock and roll. Sam Llanas of the popular Wisconsin band the BoDeans also originated from Waukesha.

Latinos today enjoy participating in community activities and community organizations and are sure to make the transition easy for the next generation of immigrants. The second and third generations are the expression of their parents' optimism and aspirations. Latinos have done well for themselves because they reflect the American values of family, faith, and work. Although Latinos share these same American values, their respective homelands did not provide them with the opportunities to express those values. The future for Latinos will always be one of hope and optimism.

Ezequiel Benavides, of a Mexican father and Texan mother, earned a bachelor of arts degree from Ohio State University, a master of arts degree from the University of Wisconsin-Madison, and taught at the University of Wisconsin-Waukesha and Carroll College in the 1960s. In 1970, the Waukesha Public Schools established a bilingual education department with Benavides as director. Benavides managed to increase the number of Latinos employed by the district and establish bilingual programs at schools. By 1975, in response to the district's freeze on hiring more bilingual personnel, Benavides resigned. Pictured above, in 1974 at a White Rock School Cinco de Mayo celebration, is Benavides.

Three-year-old Veronica San Miguel and José Acosta, aged four, were students in La Casa de Esperanza's Escuelita in the 1970s and are featured in this photograph of an Easter egg hunt. Many parents, particularly recent arrivals from Mexico, had no knowledge of many American traditions such as Halloween, the Easter rabbit, pumpkin carvings, Valentine's Day, or Easter egg hunts.

Christine Almeida (right) was born in Waco, Texas, of Mexican parents and came to Waukesha in the early 1970s, where she founded Contemporary Fitness, Inc., a health and fitness club. She was one of the first Latina entrepreneurs in Waukesha and has been an active volunteer, having served on the board of directors of the women's center and the Altrusa Club.

There were few Latino attorneys in Wisconsin before 1970. When La Casa de Esperanza received funding for its Latin American Public Defender Program, Judge Ness Flores went to the law school of the University of California-Davis and recruited two graduates from the class of 1974 to come to Waukesha. Jess Martínez (second row, center) became a Waukesha County circuit court judge, and Miguel Mitchel (first row, left) became a state public defender in Waukesha and Jefferson Counties.

Waukesha Latinos owe a debt of gratitude to Pedro Rodríguez for his tireless efforts on behalf of Latino civil rights. He was an articulate spokesman for social justice, and as La Casa de Esperanza's executive director from 1974 to 1977, he was a defender of Latino issues in government. In 1974, during hearings in the state capitol, Rodríguez (pictured above) provided testimony to the Senate Subcommittee on Education in support of the Bilingual Education Bill.

Because much of Waukesha's Mexican community has Texas roots, mariachi groups are not as common in Waukesha as they are in Mexico. However, conjuntos, bandas, and grupos musicales have appeared at social and community events for many years. Los Relativos was a popular group from the mid-1970s until the late 1990s. Pictured from left to right are (first row) Dan García and Wally Llanas; (second row) Alonzo Blanco, Pete García, and Nick Vega.

Oscar Sánchez, a longtime Waukesha resident of Mexican background, ran for Waukesha school board in April 1973. He lost the election but was appointed to the board when a vacancy developed that year. He served through April 1975, then was elected to the board and served from 1975 to 1978. He was the first Latino school board member of the Waukesha Public Schools.

The only Latino bowling league was organized by Pedro Rodríguez and Vicente de la Paz in 1975. Some of the players were beginning bowlers and used bowling as an opportunity to get together with friends. Pictured above are, from left to right, (first row) unidentified, unidentified, Ramón Ortiz, Rubén Colon, and Carlos Cintron; (second row) Manuel Cintron, Augie Maldonado, Filemón Martínez, Rubén Colon, Joe Negrón, and Paul Hernández.

The 1976 women's basketball team sponsored by La Casa de Esperanza included, from left to right, (first row) Rosalva Hernández, Cindy San Miguel, and Jackie Batteto; (second row) María Echeverría, Sylvia García, Frank San Miguel Jr., and Pedro Rodríguez; (third row) Virginia Rodríguez, Juanita San Miguel, and Elida Echeverría.

During the late 1970s and early 1980s, Carroll College intensified its recruitment of Puerto Rican students. Many remained after graduation and became community leaders. Alumnus Sonia Hernández Evans served on the board of directors of La Casa de Esperanza, has been a Waukesha Public School teacher for 30 years, and is an educational leader at the local and national level. Pictured here is Evans with her husband, Bill, and daughters Sara (left) and Marisol.

The constantly smiling face and friendly disposition of Chila Oyervides was a Waukesha fixture for many years, as she volunteered at every festival and church event. Chila and her husband, Manuel, were a highly regarded couple, were civic minded, and participated in various voter registration drives. They also were involved with LUPA (Latinos United for Political Action), a volunteer organization founded in 1980 by Dagoberto Ibarra, which promoted Latino participation in the electoral process.

Between mid-April and the end of October 1980, more than 125,000 people fled Cuba in what became known as the Mariel Boatlift. A sizeable number of *marielitos* processed through Fort McCoy settled in Wisconsin. About 20 were sponsored by various families and assisted by St. Joseph's Church in Waukesha. In 1980, Walter Sava (left), executive director of La Casa de Esperanza, greets two recent arrivals enrolling in ESL classes.

In 1980, Waukesha residents Joe Angel Medina Jr. (aged 17) and Yolanda Lomeli Medina (aged 18) were engaged when they enlisted in the United States Marine Corps under the "buddy program." Joe was an administration chief, and Yolanda was the first woman seat technician on the Harrier Jump Jet. They have since settled in Waukesha, where they raise six children and Yolanda works in the Carroll College Nursing Department. Joe became a pastor of the First Congregational Church in Genesee.

Music has always played a role in the social life of the Latino community, and from time to time Waukesha has produced several bands, conjuntos, and grupos musicales. Pedro Rodríguez and his group El Destino were popular in the late 1970s and 1980s, playing at dances in the Milwaukee area. Standing in the first row, from left to right, are José Díaz, Pedro Rodríguez, Eugenio Mesa, and Reynaldo Morones; (second row) Manuel Castillo, unidentified, Paul Camacho, Vicente Alvarez, and Jaime Balderas.

This 1981 photograph (center) of the Ibarra children, from left to right, Jessica, Lisa, and Javier, offers no clue about the accomplishments of these graduates of Escuela Preparatoria para Niños (La Casa de Esperanza's preschool). Their father, Dagoberto, served as board president of La Casa in the 1970s and 1980s and has always been a firm believer in the power of education. Lisa graduated from the University of Wisconsin-Milwaukee and is a sergeant with the Milwaukee Police Department. Jessica, a graduate of Miami University of Ohio, joined the ROTC and is currently a major in the U.S. Air Force and has served three tours of duty in Iraq. Javier earned his appointment to the Air Force Academy because of his exceptional SAT test scores. He is currently a major and has been deployed multiple times to "austere locations" in the service of his country.

In the early 1980s, Cirilo and Juana Rodríguez opened one of the first Latino grocery stores, called El Diamante. The Rodríguez family came to Waukesha from San Luis, Potosí, Mexico, in 1956, and had 10 children. Cirilo worked at Quality Aluminum for 30 years until his retirement and then ran the grocery store with the help of his family.

Ramiro and Isabel Galván represent immigrants whose search for a better life is reflected in their children's accomplishments. Ramiro came to Milwaukee from Jalisco, Mexico, and Isabel from Colombia in the 1960s. Seated are Eduardo (left), an assistant principal with Milwaukee Public Schools, and Ramiro (right), an executive with the United Way in Waukesha. Seated with Isabel is Heidi, an assistant district attorney in Milwaukee County. Standing are Adriana, a teacher at Riverside High School, and Ramiro, who retired from Wisconsin Energy Corporation after 35 years of service.

Save and Save, La Tienda Mexicana was a Waukesha fixture at the corner of White Rock and Main Street for many years, at 1002 White Rock Avenue. When Manuel Oyervides purchased the building, the first floor was used as an auction hall. In the basement, Manuel operated his television and radio repair shop. Later Manuel converted the auction business into a used furniture and appliance store. In the mid-1980s Manuel, with his wife, Chila, and family members, started Save and Save, La Tienda Mexicana. This prosperous business became a community gathering center on Sunday mornings. Manuel's business was a prime target for downtown redevelopment. As he began searching for a new location, the building burned down, and it is now the site of the Landing condominiums.

Luis Gonzáles (1929–1997) was born in San Antonio, Texas. As a disc jockey in Killeen, Texas, he became a spokesman for the Hispanic community and helped launch the careers of many legendary Tejano musicians. He came to Waukesha in the early 1980s and worked as a volunteer disc jockey on "La Voz de la Casa" on WCCX, where he often closed his show by saying "La Casa de Esperanza—no es una Esperanza—es una realidad."

Attorney Jess Martínez, from Bakersville, California, served in Southeast Asia and was discharged as a captain in 1971. He came to Wisconsin in 1974 and headed the Waukesha public defender's office from 1979 to 1982. He was the second Latino in history to have served as Waukesha County circuit judge, from 1982 to 1985. Martínez was a member of the board of directors of La Casa de Esperanza and has been in private practice for the past 20 years.

The Nicaraguan families who immigrated to Waukesha continue to maintain their tradition of family get-togethers. This late-1980s photograph includes members of the Benavente, Monterrey, and González families, as well as some of their relatives.

The Márquez brothers founded the Rockin' Robins in the mid-1970s, a band specializing in rock-and-roll classics. They have played at weddings, quinceaneras, hotels, and various parties. For many years they were very popular at Monreal's El Matador in Milwaukee. Pictured above in 1985 are, from left to right, Jimmy Kishline, Kenny Arnold, Freddy Márquez, Jerry Allen Bolgeratten, and Mario Márquez.

Richard Hernández was the best Latino campaigner in Waukesha. In addition to being the first elected Latino alderman in the history of the Waukesha Common Council, he was also the first Latino to have served on the board of the Waukesha County Technical College (WCTC). He served on the common council from 1979 until his death in 1990 and on the WCTC board from 1983 to 1989. He ran for mayor of the City of Waukesha in 1986, and although he won the primary, he lost the election. He campaigned unsuccessfully for state assembly in 1984. Hernández was a warrant officer and administrative assistant with the Wisconsin Army National Guard. He was a wonderful friend of La Casa de Esperanza and frequently bore the brunt of the racist and uncalled-for remarks of some of his fellow councilmen when matters related to La Casa came before the Waukesha Common Council.

Trino and Seferina Hernández (sitting, first row) posed for this 1989 picture with their seven children. Included, from left to right, are Helen, Anita, Inez, Jesse, Joe, María Natividad "Mary," and Elvira. Seferina, the matriarch of the family, passed away when she was 98 years old and is fondly remembered for the stories she told about the family's early years in Texas.

Born of Puerto Rican parents, Michael Reyes currently practices law in Waukesha with Ness Flores in the law firm Flores and Reyes. He is the board president of Latino Arts, Inc. His wife, Rosemary Cuevas Reyes, of Mexican and Puerto Rican parents, is a lawyer with the Wisconsin public defender's office. Both have served the community as volunteers and members of nonprofit boards and are strong proponents of diversity and a multicultural lifestyle.

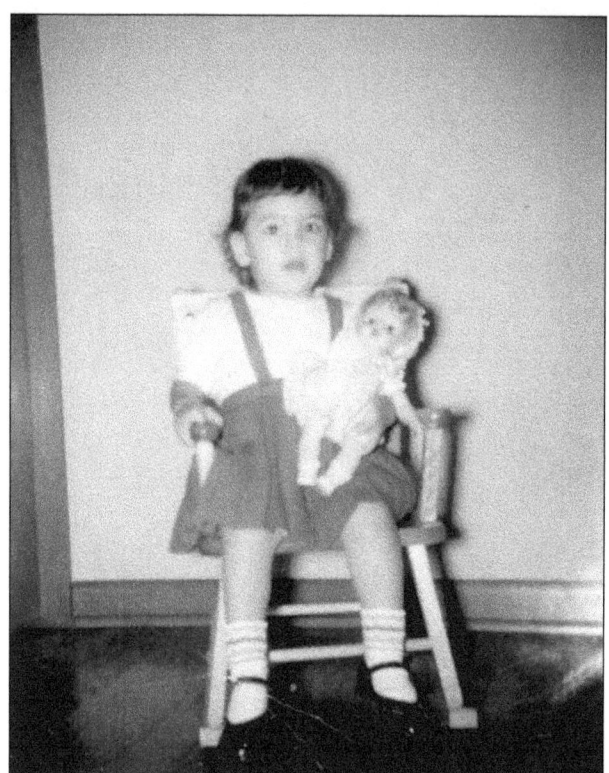

A former La Casa de Esperanza board member during the 1980s, Deborah Terrones Wallendal is a Wisconsin native whose fraternal grandparents came from Mexico. Currently the director of human resources at WCTC, Wallendal has had a long and productive history as a volunteer in Waukesha's Latino community and has the distinction of being the first Latina to have served on the board of directors of WCTC.

Inez Robert Llanas and Carmen Castillo (first row, center) are surrounded by members of their family, which includes their four children. Inez worked for the U.S. Postal Service for 26 years, and Carmen retired from the Waukesha School System after 21 years as a bilingual aide. The Llanas family was actively involved with La Casa de Esperanza, St. Joseph's Church, and the Scholastic Fund for Students of Hispanic Descent.

Carlos Gamiño (fifth from left) came to Milwaukee from Leon Guanajuato in 1967 and retired from the Waukesha Public School system after 25 years of service. In 1987, Gamiño became principal of White Rock elementary school, the first and only Latino to have served in this capacity. The employment of Latinos in the Waukesha Public Schools has always left a lot to be desired.

Few individuals have given as much of their time and talent to help nonprofit organizations as José Vásquez has over the years. Vásquez was La Casa de Esperanza board president from 1982 to 1985, and the president of the Board of the United Community Center and Latino Arts, Inc. He is the recipient of numerous awards, including Hispanic Man of the Year. During his years in Waukesha, he was the adult basic coordinator for WCTC.

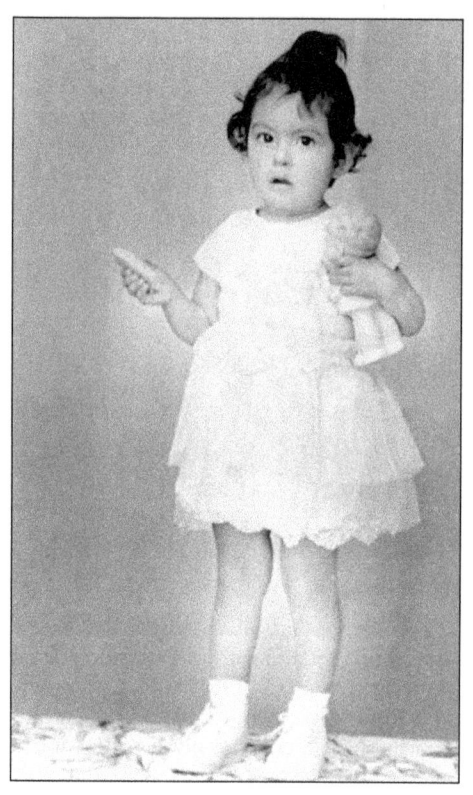

Dr. Pilar Melero came to Waukesha from Durango, Mexico, after her father, José Ramón, came here to visit a friend. While visiting, he went with his friend to a local foundry to help with a job application and was hired in the process. He then moved the family to Waukesha. Pilar received her doctorate at the University of Wisconsin-Madison. She is an assistant professor at the University of Wisconsin-Whitewater and a guest columnist for the *Milwaukee Journal Sentinel*. For several summers she helped young people at La Casa de Esperanza write and publish a newspaper, *El Aguila*.

José Cuevas was the second Latino ever to have been elected to the Waukesha School Board. He resigned in 1992 after having served for six and a half years. Cuevas came to the Milwaukee-Waukesha area from Texas in the late 1970s and was a counselor at Waukesha County Technical Institute. He was a very visible member of Waukesha's Latino community and a strong voice on the board promoting the interests of Latino families.

Gov. Tommy G. Thompson appointed Arnold A. Moncada Jr. as sheriff of Waukesha County in 1992. Elected in 1993, Moncada served for one term. He was the only Latino appointed to serve as sheriff in Wisconsin and the second Latino elected sheriff in the state. (Sheriff Fernando Pérez was the first, in Ozaukee County, and served from 1979 to 1991). Moncada retired from the Waukesha County sheriff's department in 1998, after almost 30 years of service.

This picture was taken in 1995 before Daniel Banda's PBS documentary *Mountain's Mist and Mexico* was broadcast. The film tells the story of Banda's grandparents Leonardo and Ursula immigrating to Wisconsin and his father, Reuben, obtaining the American dream. Seen by roughly five million viewers, the film created awareness of Mexican American immigrants living in the Midwest and of the immigration debate. Pictured above, from left to right, are three generations of the Bandas family: Daniel John, Joshua Daniel, and Reuben John.

Ralph Ramírez is the third Latino circuit court judge to have served and second elected in Waukesha County. Elected in 1999, Ralph (center) is pictured with his parents, Margarita and Arcadio, and Supreme Court justice Shirley Abrahamson (right). Ralph is married to Renee and has three children: Alicia, María, and Joseph. He served on the United Way Campaign, is a trustee of the Waukesha Public Library, and was a recipient of the Volunteer of the Year Award in 1998.

José Angel Negrón came to Waukesha from Puerto Rico in 1966. He is the father of four children, all of whom attended Escuelita. Negrón's voice is well known in Waukesha, where he was a volunteer disc jockey for La Casa de Esperanza's radio program *Edicion Salsera* on the Carroll College station WCCX. Negrón is one of La Casa's volunteers with the longest tenure, having volunteered his services for 25 years.

Without any doubt, Waukesha's most famous Latino musician is Sam Llanas of the BoDeans. Pictured during graduation ceremonies at Waukesha South High School in 1979 is Sam, surrounded by his father, Wally (left), and maternal grandfather, Lorenzo Sánchez. Sam developed an interest in music at an early age and began playing with various musical groups in his early 20s.

For 12 years, Dr. Elena M. De Costa has been La Casa's champion on the Carroll College campus. Of Portuguese ancestry, De Costa makes learning Spanish a "live experience" where students become involved in community projects, attend Latino cultural events, and gain firsthand knowledge of culture. She believes that classroom and community go hand in hand, and her students are the best testament of what she is able to achieve by combining theory and practice.

WCTC has had a positive relationship with Waukesha's Latino community for years. Among those who helped WCTC make inroads into the Latino community during the last 35 years are Dr. Diana González, José Vásquez, María Guadalupe Hernández, Armando García, and board members Richard Hernández and Deborah Terrones Wallendall. Current admissions specialist Manuel Santos, pictured above speaking to White Rock elementary school students, continues the tradition of recruiting Latinos for various WCTC programs.

After coming to Carroll College from Puerto Rico in the 1970s, Dr. Pablo Cardona continued his education with a doctorate from Marquette University and has become a well-regarded Latino leader in the Milwaukee area. Currently serving as vice president at Milwaukee Area Technical College (MATC), he lives in Waukesha with his wife of 29 years, Genell Gialdini. Their children Gina, Tony, and Andrew are all graduates of Catholic Memorial High School and the University of Wisconsin-Madison.

Virginia Velasco Hoeft came from Venezuela in 1973 to attend the University of Wisconsin-Waukesha, where she met her husband, Michael J. Hoeft. She graduated from Carroll College with a degree in secondary education and worked as a Spanish teacher for the Waukesha Public School District for 30 years. Pictured here is her family, from left to right, (first row) John and Emmylou; (second row) Michael, Virginia, and Andrew.

The number of Latino college graduates has dramatically increased in the past 20 years, and Latino professionals are found in almost every major corporation. Latinos are visible as owners of Mexican restaurants, but there are few Latino contractors in Waukesha. Domenico Santilli, from Venezuela, received his training at MATC and now owns Power Control. He is one of the few licensed Latino electrical contractors in the area and is optimistic about the potential growth of his company.

Ten-year-old Casa del Río is one of Waukesha's most popular restaurants. It has received excellent reviews and is setting the trend for the popularity of Mexican restaurants in the area, which at the present time number more than 10. Casa del Río is owned by Nancy Severo, Michael González, and Enrique and Rose Chacón.

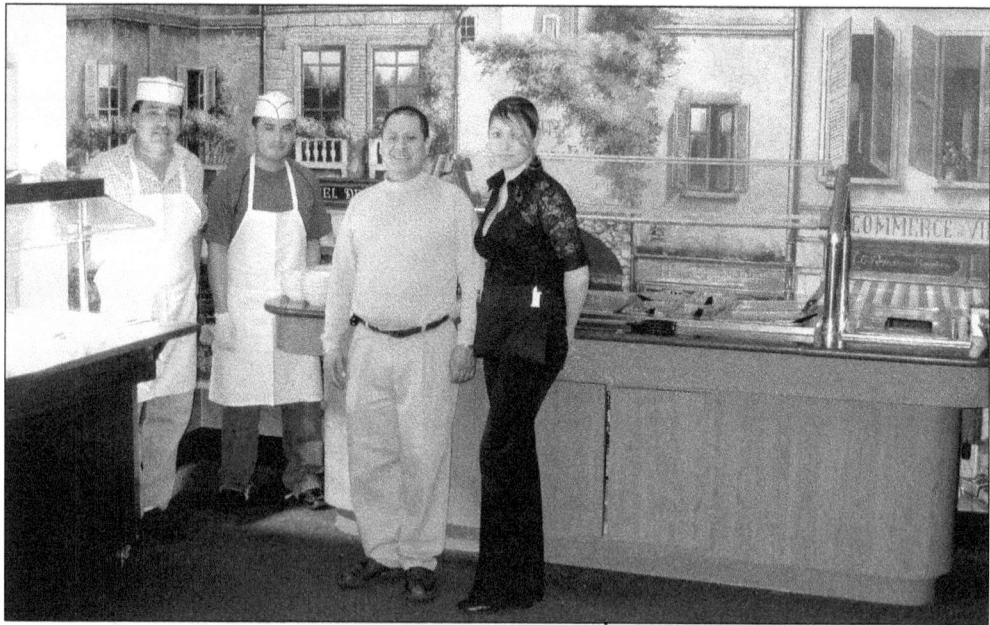

Before coming to the United States from Tejupilco, Mexico, 13 years ago, Juan León worked for the Mexican government in the penitentiaries. After living in California and then Madison, León settled in Waukesha and decided to own his own restaurant. Since 2005, he has been with El Ranchito Mexican Restaurant, which was previously owned by Jorge Saurez, María Flores, and David Gonzáles. Pictured from left to right are Francisco Candelario, José Luis Gillen, León, and his daughter, Bianca.

Irene and her husband, Antonio Reyes, have been longtime Waukesha residents. Antonio has been working with Cooper Power Systems for more than 30 years, and Irene has been the owner and operator of Styles and Belleza, a beauty salon that she started in the late 1970s. Irene's shop was among one of the first Latino-owned businesses in Waukesha. The Reyes family includes four children, including Antonio Jr., who has recently completed a tour of duty in Iraq.

Great-granddaughter of Joseph and Antonia Melendes and a fourth-generation Latina in Waukesha, Elizabeth Hernández celebrated her wedding vows at St. Joseph's Church on May 20, 2006. Her husband, Isaac Vargas, brother Christopher Hernández (second from right), and members of the wedding party are looking forward to a fifth generation of Latinos/as in the not-too-distant future.

El Rey and the Night Beats is one of the longest-running rock-and-roll bands in Wisconsin, originally playing Latin music at festivals and events. They later were one of the first rock-and-roll bands to play in Milwaukee nightclubs and will celebrate their 50th anniversary in 2007. This 1957 photograph includes, from left to right, (first row) Rusty Batelamas and Ray Ojeda; (second row) Ron Kurtz, Tom Montez, and Ace Rudan.

The Scholastic Fund for Students of Hispanic Descent, formerly the Mexican American Scholastic Fund, was founded in 1963 to award college scholarships to Waukesha high school graduates. This small group of dedicated volunteers has since awarded $114,908 to 338 students. Present board members pictured are, from left to right, (first row) Virginia Hernández (scholarship secretary) and Carmen Llanas (secretary); (second row) Inez R. Llanas (treasurer), Luis Hernández Jr. (president), and Pedro Rodríguez (vice president). Not pictured is David Alvarado.

Latino participation in the voting process continues to be a challenge. One of the biggest factors that increased Latino voter turnout during the past 30 years has been the presence of Latino candidates on the ballot. Waukesha was the first city in Wisconsin to elect Latinos to the circuit court, school board, common council, and the county board of supervisors. María Rodríguez Paz, pictured during a recent election, is one of the few Latino poll workers.

In 2007, Margarita Ramírez and Arcadio Ramírez will be celebrating their 50th wedding anniversary. Included in the wedding party above are, from left to right, Paul Llanas, Mary Pérez, Eugene Mesa, and Mary Castañeda, along with children Yolanda Casteñeda and Gilbert Rendón.

Oscar Medina was born and raised in Waukesha County, and for the past 20 years, has been working with Latino children and youth through his Medina Boxing Club and Medina Center. Pictured above, with eye patch, Medina is surrounded by youth from the University of Wisconsin Extension Leadership Program. Medina is highly regarded for his efforts to provide a disciplined environment that promotes healthy lifestyles and positive values.

Erick Cruz (far right) came with his family to Waukesha from Puerto Rico in 1996 at the age of 10. Coached by Israel Acosta (second from right) at the United Community Center, Cruz is preparing to fight in the 2008 Olympics. He has been ranked number four nationally in the Junior Olympic Division and is contemplating becoming a professional boxer.

Five

La Casa de Esperanza

Latinos had arrived and been working in Waukesha for more than 40 years before La Casa de Esperanza came into existence. In 1966, La Casa was founded by a group of non-Latino church members who, following the instructions of a Methodist pastor, were trying to change society for the better. The church group organized around the time when racial inequality, discrimination, and economic disparities were being challenged throughout the United States. Through informal research, the founders realized that existing institutions were not addressing the needs of migrant workers in and around Waukesha.

Although many workers had been recruited from Texas to work in Waukesha, the foundries that employed Latinos offered no bilingual education for them or their children. The founders also noticed that Latinos' housing was substandard and they were subject to discrimination. The founders decided to open a day care on Ryan Street, in the heart of the Spanish-speaking neighborhood the Strand. They named the organization History Builders. By 1969, many of the Latino community members began taking over the reigns of the organization, and the name History Builders was changed to La Casa de Esperanza, meaning "the House of Hope."

From the early 1970s onward, La Casa has been led by a variety of dynamic Latino leaders, ranging from those more community activist minded to those who brought tremendous growth for the organization. The boards of directors have also played a crucial role in the success of La Casa and in shaping its mission of helping Latinos achieve economic freedom and full participation in society. Its programs have concentrated on educating children and youth; finding employment, senior housing, and weatherization services; and celebrating the rich Latino history. The festival Latino Days, which had once been held on a dusty street on Ryan Street, has turned into one of Waukesha's biggest festivals, Fiesta Waukesha. Through the years, La Casa has maintained itself as the organization that Latinos go to for help, encouragement, advocacy, and most of all, hope for the future.

In 1966, Kenneth and Clair Crouch, Duane and Pat Mitchell, and Duane and Carol Warren initiated a group with the purpose of helping Latino families integrate into Waukesha's community. Today they are considered the founders of La Casa de Esperanza. One of their first activities was to purchase a community center house, pictured above at 1009 Ryan Street. It served La Casa well for 12 years, until the organization moved to the Arcadian Avenue facility.

Aline López, pictured above, served as the first Latina part-time executive director from January 1972 to August 1973. López, a mother of five, came to Waukesha in 1944 and was a very articulate and eloquent spokesperson for the Latino community at a time when advocacy for Latino issues was not only unpopular, but also viewed as "un-American."

The founders of La Casa undertook a major renovation of the Ryan Street facility. When completed, the first floor had a large classroom and a reception area. The second floor housed offices for staff and volunteers. Ricardo Díaz (far right) came to Waukesha from Puerto Rico to attend college and was executive director from 1974 to 1975. He greatly emphasized sports and youth development. It became obvious by the mid-1970s, as children and youth spilled into the front porch, that the facility needed expansion.

The name La Casa de Esperanza, Inc., went through evolutionary stages. It was first established as History Builders, Inc., and also referred to as the Ryan Street Neighborhood House. By 1969, a sign was placed above the main entrance with the name Casa de Esperanza. In 1971, the name was formalized as La Casa de Esperanza. Pictured above is the building at the time it was sold in 1979 to a church group for $45,000.

María García San Miguel Benavides, the intellectual mother of La Casa de Esperanza, moved to Waukesha from Texas with her family in the 1940s. She was frequently applauded for her excellent English, but having lived in Waukesha most her life, Benavides considered such comments racist. She helped start Escuela Preparatoria para Niños, was on the first board of directors of La Casa, and served as La Casa's assistant executive director from 1978 to 1980.

The 1978 La Casa Board of Directors included 16 individuals. Pictured above are, from left to right, (first row) Sonia Hernández Evans, Ricardo Díaz, Diane de la Santos, Dolores Pérez Karner, and Sylvia García; (second row) Francisco Ríos, Dagoberto Ibarra, Fr. Larry Dulek, Albert Lehr, John Doran, and Fred Moss. Not pictured are Sonia Treviño, María Blong, Armando Bras, Cristóbal Díaz, and Fátima Muniain.

Día de la Comunidad Latina, or Latino Community Day, was first celebrated in August 1977 and underwent a gradual growth and development. It initially took place in front of La Casa at 1009 Ryan Street. The following year La Casa moved its headquarters and the festival was moved to Arcadian Avenue. The event began with a three-mile run, mass at St. Joseph's, and a procession from the church to La Casa. It culminated with a street festival that included food, dances, and cultural activities. Pictured above are, from left to right, Martin Mata, Virginia Rodríguez, and Valentina Mata. (Courtesy of the Waukesha County Historical Society and Museum.)

Fr. Larry Dulek was pastor of St. Joseph's Church and an active La Casa board member during the late 1970s and early 1980s. He was an outspoken and beloved leader for Waukesha's Latino community. Pictured here are, from left to right, Fr. Donald Richardson, Archbishop Rembert Weakland, and Fr. Larry Dulek as they celebrate mass during La Casa's Día de la Comunidad Latina on Arcadian Avenue in 1978.

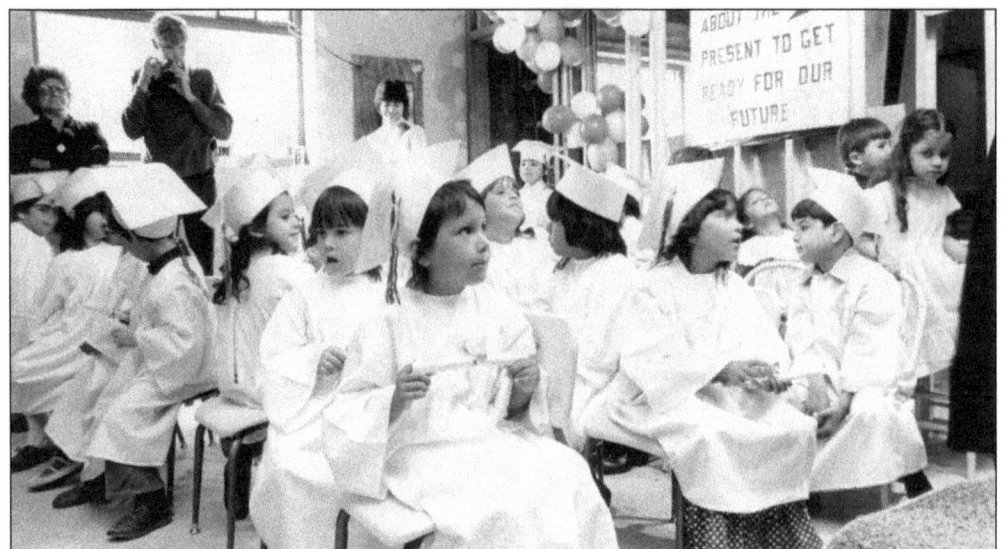

Escuela Preparatoria para Niños was established as a preschool program in 1966. It started with about 20 children at the Schutze Building and moved to the First United Methodist Church. With assistance from United Way, it merged with La Casa de Esperanza in 1975. It is currently known as Escuelita and has an enrollment of more than 250 children. It is housed in a $3.5 million state-of-the-art facility that was inaugurated in 2001.

Carmen de la Paz has been associated with La Casa for about 40 years. She began teaching at Escuela Preparatoria para Niños in 1971, shortly after the organization was founded. She eventually became coordinator of the entire preschool operation and continues to be involved at La Casa as a volunteer. Pictured above, at the First United Methodist Church, is de la Paz with her students in 1978, the last year that Escuelita operated out of rented facilities.

The original two La Casa buildings at 410 Arcadian Avenue were purchased for $60,000 and consisted of an office building (left) and a warehouse (right). During the search for new headquarters it was Jean Batha, working with a real estate firm, who helped La Casa purchase these buildings. Waukesha State Bank provided a $20,000 mortgage to complete the purchase. The office building only had around 2,000 feet of usable space, with a garage in the back of the building. The warehouse was in total disrepair, unheated, and a neighborhood eyesore.

As soon as La Casa moved into the Arcadian Avenue facility, it began remodeling the back part of the office building garage. Once the doors were removed, it was necessary to build a foundation for the proposed extension. Several youth were employed through the CETA (Comprehensive Employment and Training Act) summer youth employment program. Pictured above in the front trench with shovel in hand is Joe Rodríguez, one of the program participants.

Remodeling of the Gittner Coal and Supply Company's 6,000-square-foot warehouse, including exterior lighting, parking, and landscaping, was determined to cost about $300,000. The La Casa de Esperanza board approved a plan to remodel the upstairs into two classrooms for Escuelita, which was renting space at the First United Methodist Church, and to convert the first floor into a community room and senior center with a kitchen.

On April 29, 1979, La Casa held an open house at its new Arcadian Avenue facilities. Thanks to the help received from Frank Hedgecock with the City of Waukesha and the support of Mayor Joseph C. LaPorte, La Casa received two Community Development Block Grants of $65,000 each. The grants were used to contract with Link Builders to remodel the buildings. Pictured above are Judge Ness Flores (left) and La Casa executive director Walter Sava (right) as they unveil plans for the renovation of the warehouse and office building.

Pictured at right in 1980 is Century Fence president Anthony W. Bryant (left) and Flores (right) upon receiving a $30,000 grant from the Kresge Foundation, which completed the $250,000 capital campaign for the La Casa renovation. Earlier that year, Flores met with Kresge officials in Troy, Michigan. When asked if he was familiar with the Michigan area, Flores replied, "My family and I worked in the fields in the Troy area for several summers."

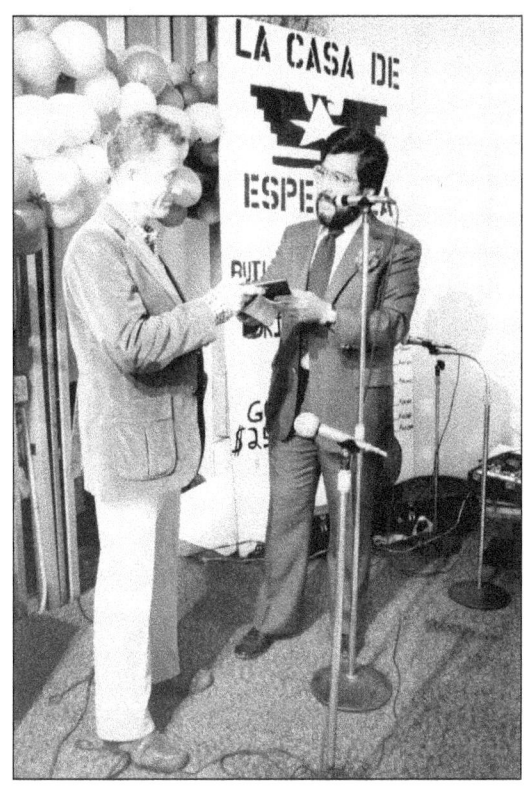

When cable television came to Waukesha in the late 1970s, RVS Cable won the franchise, with the condition that community groups had access to public programming. RVS made its studios and equipment available to La Casa for the production of a weekly television show. *Mural Latino*, hosted by Delia Couto Sava (pictured above) aired twice a week. The program lasted about two years, until new owners of cable television in Waukesha discontinued all Latino outreach efforts.

The Marchan brothers, Lupe, Evaristo, José, and Francisco, have all been very involved in Waukesha's Latino community, particularly at St. Joseph's Church and La Casa de Esperanza. José, pictured above with his son Gabriel, served as cochair of Día de la Comunidad Latina for many years in the late 1970s and was a strong proponent of preserving and sharing the Latino culture.

After the renovation of La Casa's headquarters and community center was completed, La Casa received a grant from the Wisconsin Arts Board, which allowed it to hire Chicano artist Carlos Rosas to paint a large 20-by-100-foot mural on the side of the building and a small mural on the front.

The Carlos Rosas mural on the side of the Community Center/Escuelita in 1980 had a variety of symbols and reminders of the Latino culture. One half was especially attractive and included a portrait of Judge Ness Flores, the original La Casa building, and other details. By the time Rosas painted the second half, the weather had turned colder, and he ended up painting three very large figures without the details included in the first half.

Remodeling of the warehouse was completed on budget and on time. Not only had La Casa successfully completed its $250,000 capital campaign, it also received assistance from the Milwaukee Seabeas, who did most of the second-floor remodeling for the preschool. In June 1981, the Seabeas (pictured above) stand as the honor guard for the graduated Escuelita class of 1981.

Among the various activities included in the Día de la Comunidad/Latino Community Day program was a parade from St. Joseph's Church to La Casa de Esperanza. Leading the 1980 parade were Don Genaro Castillo, María Soto, and Norma Villareal, carrying the Puerto Rican flag.

Carol and Duane Warren (at the podium) have not been disappointed by the investment they made in La Casa. On the contrary, over the years they have continued to generously support La Casa's mission. In 1980, when La Casa held its first annual dinner at the Waukesha Holiday Inn, it was publicly recognized for making such a huge difference in the lives of many Latinos.

Sonia Treviño served on La Casa's board of directors in the 1970s and 1980s and was a frequent volunteer and advocate for Latino community events. An outspoken activist, her English fluency was sometimes questionable, especially when unsure of certain terms. Members of a United Way panel were treated to a linguistic gaffe when Treviño proclaimed that Waukesha Latinos needed "up your mobility," when she meant upward mobility.

Manuel Flores came to Waukesha from Texas in 1966 and has not stopped working since. In addition to his 32 years of service at Wisconsin Centrifugal (Metal Tech), he has been a driver at Dairyland Bus Company. He has been named an outstanding volunteer at La Casa de Esperanza for his 16 years as the volunteer disc jockey of *La Voz de la Casa*, a four-hour Sunday morning program on WCCX, a Carroll College radio station.

Under Dagoberto Ibarra's leadership in the 1970s, La Casa de Esperanza grew to be a leading social service agency. Members of La Casa's board of directors posed for this 1980 photograph. Pictured are, from left to right, (first row) president Dagoberto Ibarra, vice president Debbie Terrones, treasurer Manuel Lugo, secretary José Olivieri, Angel Basabe, and Armando Bras; (second row) Jess Martínez, Lupe Barreto, Ricardo Díaz, Diana González, Rick Congdon, Edgardo Ocasio, José Vásquez, and Inga Villarreal.

In 1981, city officials informed La Casa that Latino Community Day festival had to be moved because the State of Wisconsin Department of Transportation would not close Arcadian Avenue, Highway 59. Instead the event took place in the back lot of La Casa under very uncomfortable conditions. Thus began a series of different venues, including the park behind the YMCA and the University of Wisconsin-Waukesha campus. None of these venues were very successful until La Casa moved the festival to its current Frame Park location in 1986.

René Farías came to work at La Casa in 1982 as an employment specialist. He rose through the ranks, eventually becoming executive director from 1990 to 1992. Originally from Baja, California, Farías displayed keen insights into the plight of the Mexican immigrant and is an eloquent exponent of the assimilation process and its consequences. An able administrator, he strengthened the bases for La Casa's future building expansion.

As Waukesha's Latino community grew and La Casa received increased recognition, elected officials began to court the Hispanic vote. From left to right are Sen. Gaylord Nelson, Mayor Joseph C. LaPorte, Judge Ness Flores, and Carmen Hernández, a teacher in Escuelita. LaPorte was the non-Latino elected official most helpful to La Casa in the organization's history. He helped revitalize the Strand area and aided in La Casa's purchase and renovation of the Arcadian Avenue facility.

Most social events that La Casa de Esperanza has sponsored over the years have relied heavily on the support of volunteers. Latino Community Days/Fiesta Waukesha has been especially blessed by hundreds of volunteers who have helped ensure the success of the event. Pictured at left is Viola Lomeli. She came to Waukesha in the 1950s from Laredo, Texas, and recently retired from Waukesha Memorial Hospital after more than 30 years of service.

Waukesha's Latino community embraced Latino Community Day with great enthusiasm. The festival later became Latino Community Days, when the celebration expanded into a three-day event. In 1986, it became Fiesta Waukesha, held at Frame Park.

Fred Gutiérrez was born in Puerto Rico. He joined La Casa in 1979 as a benefits specialist for the elderly and later became executive director from 1983 to 1990. During this period, the La Casa Village Apartments were completed, Fiesta Waukesha started in Frame Park, and the expansion of programs eventually doubled the agency's budget. He later joined the Greater Milwaukee Foundation, becoming the first Latino program officer in a major foundation in the Milwaukee area.

Graduation ceremonies at Escuelita were not only a community gathering, but also a family event, particularly for Carmen de la Paz (pictured above, far right). The children, and especially the parents, were pleased to receive a graduation diploma, which read, "This is to certify that (name of child) has graduated from Escuela Preparatoria para Niños with the ability to learn, play, and go to kindergarten in the Fall."

Career Exploration through Theater Production was the name of the project that allowed La Casa de Esperanza to hire young people in the summer of 1980, pay them a small stipend, and teach a variety of skills such as acting, carpentry, electricity, painting, and costume design. Under the direction of Prof. David Molthen of Carroll College, this turned out to be a wonderful experience for the young people involved.

In the early 1980s, Diana Mesa was the coordinator for La Casa's summer recreation program. More than 100 children participated in the six-week program, which included one week of camp activities and five weeks of recreational activities.

Very few entities in Waukesha County have been as helpful to La Casa as the YWCA. Under the leadership of then executive director Beverly Chappie, the YWCA made its facilities available for five weeks to more than 100 of La Casa's children for the summer recreation program. Not only did they provide the facilities, but also staff assistance to make the summer program a truly memorable experience.

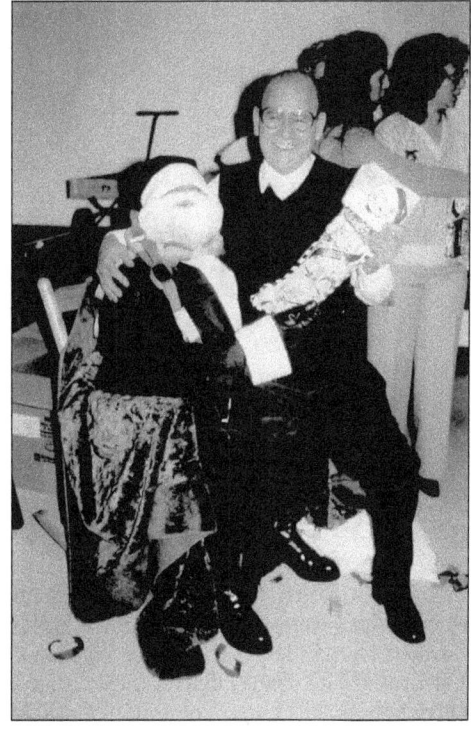

Don Cristóbal Díaz, longtime board member of La Casa and board treasurer in the early 1980s, was an active supporter of La Casa's efforts to provide programs and activities for elderly Latinos. In addition, he frequently volunteered at Escuelita and even enjoyed the perks of working with preschoolers, a visit with Santa.

Several students who came to Carroll College from Puerto Rico developed their leadership skills during their time as volunteers at La Casa de Esperanza. Pictured in 1985 during the grand opening of La Casa Village are, from left to right, Edgar Ocasio, Rafi Aguilo, and José Olivieri. Both Ocasio and Olivieri served in the 1980s as presidents of La Casa's board of directors.

By 1985, La Casa had grown to almost 50 employees. Pictured above are managers and assistants whose offices were in La Casa's office building. The employees featured are, from left to right, Carmen Hernández, María Coto, Carmen de la Paz, René Farías, Andrés Guzmán, Mary Well, Valentina Mata, Sandy Barrera, executive director Fred Gutiérrez, Mary Gray, Tony Méndez, Larry Schalk, Luz López, Jorge López, and María Banks.

When La Casa announced in 1982 that it had received a Housing and Urban Development grant for $2.6 million to build elderly housing, it was totally unaware of the hateful response it would receive from the neighbors of the proposed apartment complex. La Casa made an offer to purchase land by Sunset Avenue, which needed to be annexed to the City of Waukesha and rezoned. There were a series of hearings and meetings at city hall from February to April 1983, during which several aldermen showed their disdain for Waukesha's Latino community. The *Waukesha Freeman* reported on February 25, 1983, that neighbors believed the project would "ghetto-ize" the area. On April 8, the *Milwaukee Journal* reported that "Alderman Thomas Owens, Common Council President, had presented the alderman with a petition signed by more than 100 people who objected to the project. He said he agreed with the opposition." The Waukesha Common Council reluctantly gave approval after La Casa threatened a civil rights lawsuit. In 1985, the 51-unit elderly housing complex La Casa Village was inaugurated. Pictured are, from left to right, former executive director Walter Sava, board president Dagoberto Ibarra, executive director Fred Gutiérrez, and future executive director René Farías. La Casa Village was later expanded by 20 units in 2002.

The annual dinners of La Casa de Esperanza are a wonderful way to acknowledge donors, recognize volunteers, and provide a platform for prominent Latinos to share their insights and personal philosophies about the status of the Latino community. Carlos Romero Barcelo, the governor of Puerto Rico, was the invited guest speaker at the 31st annual dinner in 1997. He is pictured with Nancy Hernández (left) and her daughter Elizabeth (right).

Anselmo Villarreal has been the driving force behind La Casa de Esperanza's dramatic growth during the last 15 years. Anselmo became executive director in 1992, and under his leadership the agency expanded its program and facilities, especially its preschool program Escuelita. This program has been a showcase for La Casa and is frequently visited by educators and dignitaries. This 1998 photographs shows visitors, along with Gov. Lee Sherman Dreyfus (far right), interacting with the children.

Harry Quadracci is pictured holding an award from La Casa, recognizing his generous support in meeting the needs of the Waukesha Hispanic community. Anselmo Villarreal often reminisces about the call he received at his home on the eve of the Kresge challenge grant deadline. Quadracci had called to ask if he needed to provide additional support for the campaign to be successfully completed. This is only one example of the generous support and friendship Quadracci and Quad/Graphics have shared with La Casa over the years.

La Casa executive directors who have served between 1978 and the present are pictured at a "board meeting" celebrating "Tequila Month." Shown from left to right are Walter Sava, Ph.D. (1978–1983), Fred Gutiérrez (1983–1990), René Farías (1990–1992), and Anselmo Villarreal (1992–present). Other executive directors include Aline López (1972–1973), Ricardo Díaz (1974–1975), and Pedro Rodríguez (1975–1977).

Martin H. "Marty" Frank and Anselmo Villarreal stand side by side on May 25, 2000, at the ceremonial groundbreaking for La Casa de Esperanza's new community center. Marty is a longtime friend and supporter of La Casa, the president of Waukesha State Bank, and the chairman of the $2.3 million capital campaign that made the community center a reality. He also became the chairperson of the La Casa de Esperanza Foundation, established in 2003.

The chairman, president, and CEO of HUSCO International, Agustín "Gus" Ramírez, is surrounded by family members and representatives from La Casa de Esperanza at the inauguration of La Casa's new facilities. The Colonel Agustín A. Ramírez and Gloria A. Ramírez Multipurpose Room is named in honor of Gus's parents. He and his wife, Becky, have been generous supporters to causes in the Milwaukee area and parts of Central and South America.

Anselmo Villarreal presents Tony and Andrea Bryant with the Corporate Citizens of the Year award at La Casa's 35th anniversary celebration in November 2001. Looking on in the center is Martin H. Frank. The Bryants have received numerous other awards as recognition for their various volunteer and philanthropic efforts. Andrea became a member of the La Casa de Esperanza Foundation in 2003 and cochaired La Casa's $2.5 million capital campaign from 2005 to 2007.

Café Esperanza, the newest program addition at La Casa de Esperanza, was inaugurated in 2006. In addition to preparing all the meals for the children in Escuelita, Café Esperanza serves as a job-training site and, given the popularity of Mexican food, has become a well-liked destination for area residents. Pictured above are, from left to right, chef Elvira Prado, Carla Prado, Guadalupe Rodríguez, Rafael Cardoso, and Arturo Jiménez.

The La Casa Weatherization Program began in 1979 with a budget of $200,000 and a staff of mostly trainees. Initially the program aimed to reduce energy costs of low-income households and through CETA, train individuals to become weatherization specialists. By the mid-1980s, the focus shifted to strictly energy conservation. Under the leadership of Andrés Guzmán, Weatherization Services has become the largest program at La Casa, in terms of budget, number of employees, and quality of work. It has grown dramatically and provides services in three counties: Milwaukee, Jefferson, and Waukesha. With a budget of about $12 million, it provided services to almost 2,000 units of housing in 2006.

Visit us at
arcadiapublishing.com